Companion Planting

Companion Planting

Organic Gardening Tips and
Tricks for Healthier, Happier Plants

ALLISON GREER

Photographs by Tim Greer

Skyhorse Publishing

Skyhorse Publishing books may be purchased in bulk
at special discounts for sales promotion, corporate
gifts, fund-raising, or educational purposes.
Special editions can also be created to specifications.
For details, contact the Special Sales Department,
Skyhorse Publishing, 307 West 36th Street, 11th Floor,
New York, NY 10018 or info@skyhorsepublishing.com.

Skyhorse® and Skyhorse Publishing® are
registered trademarks of Skyhorse Publishing, Inc.®,
a Delaware corporation.

Visit our website at www.skyhorsepublishing.com.

10 9 8 7 6 5 4 3 2 1

Library of Congress Cataloging-in-Publication Data is
available on file.

Cover design by Qualcom

Hardcover ISBN: 978-1-62914-171-8
Paperback ISBN: 978-1-5107-4259-8
Ebook ISBN: 978-1-5107-4260-4

Printed in China

CONTENTS

This book is dedicated to my husband, Tim. He has encouraged my gardening habit from the beginning and was always at the ready for any project I suggested. During the writing of this book, I was supplied with warm dinners, clean clothes, and endless encouragement.

Thank You.

ACKNOWLEDGMENTS

My editor, Abigail Gehring, who had the foresight to envision this book, and who believed in my ability to write its words.

The following gardeners, farmers, family and friends who allowed us to stop by their gardens for photos. We talked about gardens and gardening, swapped ideas, and shared in our excitement for the natural world.

Susan Cerny & Adam Reed of Tangleroot Farm

Joe & Cathy Dello Stritto

Becky Gates

Bob & Ruth Greer

Chris & Aaren Harris of Wing Road Farm

Casey & Kelly Holzworth of Kelsey's Quarter Acre Farm

Ralph, Susan, & Christopher Kaiser

Phipps Conservatory and Botanical Gardens

Erika Tebbens of Little Sparrow Farm

My mother, Jean Brew, who graciously loaned me her laptop for three months so I could finish writing.

Our garden helper, Kevin Brew, who helped us plant, trellis, and harvest during the 2013 season.

My father, Robert Brew, who built us a chicken run so the chickens would stop tearing up the garden.

My father-in-law, Robert Greer, who's spent the last 50 years cramming apple trees and plants into his kitchen garden, and who inspires us every time we visit.

Hassan Lopez. When I first discussed the possibility of this book, he told me that I just "had" to write it. I don't know if I would have otherwise.

Tatiana Zarnowski, who willingly read over and edited earlier drafts of my manuscripts, and offered excellent advice.

All my gardening friends in the online world who've stopped by my blog to share in my enthusiasm.

Chapter 1

AN INTRODUCTION TO COMPANION PLANTING

On Growing Things

Despite all the practicality of modern convenience, watching something edible grow still possesses a delicate magic that can't be replicated in the grocery store. Every time I talk to people about gardening, they either profess their love for growing things, or they see gardening as something beyond the realm of possibility. In all cases, people appear to recognize the majesty of a simple garden.

I designed this book for the kitchen gardener. A kitchen gardener is an individual who cultivates a garden to provide for his or her family and to enrich the family diet. The kitchen garden is so named because it is often situated near the house and can provide most of the family's vegetables and fruits.

I recognize that most of you who pick up this book may also work full time. Like the typical American, you probably work at a job that demands a good portion of your waking hours. Perhaps you've looked to gardening for some stress relief, or to economize; maybe you've turned to gardening to refocus your priorities. Maybe you've begun to reject the industrialized food system and are hoping to produce a wholesome, organic, homegrown alternative. Whatever the reason, my goal is to shape your understanding of gardening into a fulfilling yet manageable component of your daily life—a bit of daily magic.

On Companion Planting

My definition of companion planting is very basic, and perhaps more generic than the traditional understanding.

Companion Planting—*Plant many things. Mix them up—plant herbs, vegetables, and flowers together. Watch them grow.*

There's more to discuss. I still have to tell you about soil, and bugs, and chemicals (never, ever, ever). Still, the definition I've provided sums up my approach to gardening fairly well.

Creating an environment where flowers, edibles, and herbs all intermingle describes a version of companion planting that is approachable to newer gardeners, those who garden in tiny spaces, and those with room to spare.

If you've decided to grow an organic garden, companion planting offers a way for you to grow healthy and resilient plants without relying on harmful chemicals for their survival. Companion planting is ideal for kitchen gardeners, because all of your plants will be flung together in a beautiful configuration.

The companion planting techniques described in this book are based on the understanding that both above and below the surface of the soil, plants interact. It is clear that plants do not exist in nature in isolation. Every aspect of plant production is dependent on some level of cooperation with the surrounding plants, insects, and microbes in the soil.

Above the soil's surface, it is undoubtedly observable that some flowers attract pollinators to the garden. Bee balm is a magnet for honeybees, an aromatic delight for their instinctive nectar and pollen collecting habit. While the honeybees may initially be drawn to the garden by bee balm flowers, they'll also visit the flowering blossoms of the tomato. Flowers may initially appear superfluous to the average vegetable farmer, but the presence of flowers attracts beneficial pollinators to the garden in general.

Many plant combinations offer a multitude of benefits, and my reasoning for companion planting follows that approach. For instance, some may scoff at the garden lore that the presence of borage can improve the flavor of tomatoes. That idea is somewhat subjective and difficult to substantiate. However, borage does attract hornworms away from tomato plants. Therefore, while the first reason for interplanting borage and tomatoes cannot be substantiated with evidence, the latter can. If borage can deter hornworms and also improve the flavor of tomatoes, well, that's even better. I'll collect the hornworms to feed our chickens, and the tomatoes and borage flowers will go in my salad.

It's also been shown and corroborated by scientific evidence that insects interact with other insects. For example, even a first year gardener has witnessed that same tomato hornworm, burdened by parasitic wasps, munching on its last tomato leaf before it succumbs to the larvae, shrivels, and dies. I sighed with dismay the first time I saw aphids on my tomatillo leaves, but two days later, the ladybugs were there to collect their lunch. In fact, it's estimated that 95 percent of insects in the garden are beneficial, and many of them are predatory.

Plants also communicate with each other. Some of these actions are not as observable to the gardener, because they cannot be seen with the naked eye. For instance, if a tomato plant has been attacked by a pest, it secretes a chemical to warn the other tomato plants that an attack is imminent. The fragrance of the chemical secreted by the attacked plant will send a message to the other neighboring plants. Those plants will then produce chemicals that are actually toxic to the pests.

In other cases, a plant can reduce its own damage by changing the taste of its leaves. Once the leaves have been chewed, the plant will collect bitter compounds to make the leaves unappealing to pests. Beneficial insects don't generally chew on leaves, and they won't be deterred by the bitterness.

Scientists, and even some gardeners, often dismiss any companion planting as simple storytelling, a folktale woven by optimistic and naive gardeners. It is true that companion planting techniques are difficult to re-create in a controlled environment for specific scientific analysis. There are incalculable variables that can influence a plant's growth. However, there have been numerous scientific studies devoted to specific plant combinations, and many of those studies have confirmed the long-held observations of companion gardeners.

While scientists have not been able to test every specific plant combination (even the possibilities are intimidating), it is clear that plants benefit from the companionship of other plants. That's how plants have grown since the beginning of time. Plants, insects, and microbes in nature interact—every living organism interacts—and sometimes that interaction hurts, but most of the time it helps. To ignore that collaboration in your backyard garden by planting each crop in a separate bed, in a neat little row, with large swaths of bare soil, is to ignore nature's lesson. Forests and prairies do not have neat little rows of monocropped vegetation, or bare floors swept clean from debris. No wonder backyard gardeners are constantly battling insects that swoop in to feast on the unprotected plants. Most pests are attracted by smell and taste. When we present our little edibles exposed in the garden unprotected, it's as though we're serving them up on a platter.

When companion planted beds are established in a garden, the level of insect life—of both beneficials and pests—increases exponentially. Even though the number of pests you see may escalate, the damage and destruction you'll observe will lessen greatly. Plant pests will become confused by the multitude of smells and tastes, and it will make it more challenging for them to find their favorite plant to munch. By mimicking nature through companion planting, you encourage biodiversity and create a mini ecosystem within your backyard. The opportunity for a singular pest to overtake that ecosystem is not present.

In fact, it is strange and curious that the agricultural sciences have chosen to pursue herbicides, fungicides, pesticides, chemical fertilizers, and genetic modification rather than attempt to emulate nature's defense system. Because all of these techniques run contrary to nature, they are all doomed to eventual failure. Unfortunately, short-term economic gain often supersedes a concern for our collective environmental health.

Outside of its ability to create a healthier garden ecosystem, companion planting also offers gardeners with limited room a chance to expand the selection of edibles they can produce. Interplanting vegetables, flowers, and herbs in a single garden bed offers a plethora of benefits that reaches far beyond pest control. Reducing the available bare space around plants creates a hot and humid environment beneath the plant leaves, and the environment makes weed germination unlikely. The shelter those leaves offer forms a habitat for beneficial predators and parasites.

Varying plants by height provides shade for plants that would be too hot on their own. Lettuce will last in the garden much longer if it's nestled in the shade of a larger leafy vegetable.

Plants also vary in their root depth. Through interplanting, a gardener could combine a plant that possesses a shallow root system with one that generates a deep root structure. The plants will be able to inhabit the same space without competing for nutrients. The varied root structure will also aerate the soil.

Science has demonstrated that legumes, like peas and beans, "fix" nitrogen to their roots, and that the nitrogen accumulated will aid the ravenous roots of "heavy feeder" crops that have been established nearby. As legumes actually add nutrients to the soil, a companion gardener might combine the legumes with an edible that depends on a high level of nutrients to thrive. With an awareness of the differing demands of varying plants, companion planting seeks to maintain a nutrient balance in the soil.

In some cases, gardeners hoping for complementary plant combinations might inadvertently design a scenario that encourages plant competition. Some plants can inhibit the growth of their neighbors. Wormwood, the plant origin

of absinthe, is known to emit chemicals that kill or stunt the growth of neighboring plants. It has been well documented that black walnut trees exhibit similar properties. Juglone, the staining dye of the black walnut, has been identified as the toxic chemical. Like wormwood and black walnut trees, some plant roots will emit chemicals that reduce the productivity of particular plant neighbors. This protective nature of plants is called allelopathy. The chemical process allows plants to establish territory and stake their ground before a competitor moves in. Sometimes a plant will emit an allelopathic chemical while it is living, and others will as they decompose.

Beyond all the other reasons provided for companion planting, it must be understood that a companion planted garden is quite beautiful. Single file plants are neat and organized, but they're a bit boring. The haphazard nature of a companion planted kitchen garden is much more romantic in its design.

———————

To devise a companion planted garden that meets your needs, start with the plant combinations I've suggested. The bed designs I've drawn are based on scientific studies, and the steady observations of gardeners over many generations, including my own. They can be scaled smaller or larger, depending upon the space you have available. It is my sincere hope that even those of you who claim only a tiny patch of earth will still find this book useful. If you have only a sunlit balcony, or a tiny strip of space

between the porch and the sidewalk, you can still grow something. Throughout these pages, I offer options for those of you limited by space.

Companion planting does necessitate more planning and forethought than a traditional garden, but by emulating nature, and designing a micro ecosystem for the kitchen garden in the backyard, you will find your garden much less troubled by diseases and pests, and you will spend most of your time in the garden harvesting, transplanting, and seeding new crops.

Chapter 2

THE PRINCIPLES OF COMPANION PLANTING

The central understanding at the heart of companion planting is that an organic garden can thrive and flourish when nature is emulated, and interaction is encouraged and supported—not ignored or suppressed.

A successfully planted organic garden won't have the same appearance as a conventional garden. A chemically dependent garden can be planted in tidy rows because the chemicals will keep pests and diseases somewhat in check. However, the apparent sterility and organization of a chemically dependent garden is deceiving.

At first glance, my companion planted beds might seem a bit random in their organization. There aren't many neat rows, bare soil, or hard edges. However, my

Kale with coneflowers

beds are organized—they're organized *conceptually* by the following five fundamental principles.

Principle 1: Crop Rotation

Switching the crops grown in your beds every year will disorient soil-dwelling pests and reduce the impact of any diseases that have lain in wait for an edible's return. Tomatoes are notoriously susceptible to a wide assortment of diseases, including fusarium wilt, verticillium wilt, and bacterial wilt. Those diseases can overwinter in the earth, and they will feast on your tomato plants each year, as long as they can find them in the soil. However, if the tomatoes migrate from bed to bed like transient gypsies, the diseases will languish, and the pests will starve and die off. When planning your garden, try to rotate crop families so that a repeat family is planted in the same bed only every four years. This can be frustratingly difficult if you have a small space. The garden space, however small, should be divided into at least 4 or 6 sections so that efficient crop rotation is possible.

Botanical Plant Families

Plant family classification is often useful because many plant families suffer damage from similar pests and benefit from the same plant companions. Growing conditions are also often comparable.
Plant families often have several aliases. In the chart below, I tried to mention most of the plant family name variations you might come across in your research. The names I've chosen to use in this book are italicized.

Not all plants fit into a neat little family plant chart. Asparagus has been classified as almost a standalone crop. Corn is a member of the grass family, but most other grasses are not grown in a typical kitchen garden.

Alliums (Liliaceae) Lily family	Chives, garlic, garlic chives, leeks, onions, scallions, shallots
Asters (Asteraceae) Sunflower family	Chicory, lettuce, Jerusalem artichokes, sunflowers
Brassicas (Brassicaceae) Cole crops, cabbage family, mustard family, crucifers	Arugula, broccoli, Brussels sprouts, cabbage, cauliflower, collards, garden cress, kale, kohlrabi, horseradish, mustard, radishes, rutabaga, turnips
Carrot (Apiaceae/Umbelliferae) Parsley family	Caraway, carrots, celery, chervil, cilantro, dill, fennel, lovage, parsley, parsnips, Queen Anne's Lace
Cucurbits (Cucurbitaceae) Squash family	Cantaloupes, cucumbers, summer squash, winter squash, pumpkins, watermelons, zucchini
Legumes (Fabaceae)	Beans, peas, peanuts
Nightshade Tomato family	Eggplants, ground cherries, tomatoes, peppers, potatoes, tomatillos
Spinach (Chenopodiaceae) Goosefoot family	Beets, Swiss chard, spinach

Crop rotation also encourages a balanced level of nutrients in each bed. If the same crops, or crops from the same family, are planted in a bed year after year, the produce harvested will diminish in size, quality, and productivity. While some crops, like cabbage or corn, "heavily feed" from plant beds, others, like peas or beans, replenish the soil. By rotating the crops each year, nutrients will rebuild, and soil will sustain a reasonable level of nutrient density. With that in mind, try not to repetitively plant heavy feeders in the same bed season after season.

The root depth of various crops differs drastically. Radishes and spinach have relatively shallow roots (around 12 inches). By comparison, the roots of a squash plant can dig down as far as 6 feet. Deep taproots pull buried nutrients up from the soil. They will travel much deeper than any "double-digger," and they won't require a shovel. They exemplify how your plants can work the soil for you without you ever having to deeply till.

Green tomatoes and borage

Rosemary with petunias

Depth in Feet	Crop
1	Radishes and spinach
1 to 2	Garlic, onions, lettuce, peas, summer squash, strawberries
1.5 to 2.5	Turnips
2	Cabbage, cauliflower, celery, cucumber, eggplant, green beans
2 to 3	Artichokes, carrots, peppers, potatoes, sweet potatoes, watermelons
3	Cantaloupe and tomatoes
3 to 4	Melons and pumpkins
3 to 5	Beets
4	Lima beans
6	Asparagus , sweet corn, and Swiss chard

Through crop rotation, plant beds have access to all kinds of root depth, and the deeper taproots will aerate the soil on a rotating basis. If plants with different root depths are paired with each other, they won't compete for the same nutrients, and their varied rooting patterns will utilize the space more resourcefully. If crop roots aren't in competition, the plants can also be seeded more intensively.

Principle 2: Interplant

Let's be clear. When I use the term "interplant," I'm not referring to a bed of cab-bage with a few marigolds decoratively arranged at either end. When I interplant, each bed generally contains between five and seven crops, flowers, or herbs, and by strategically considering their varied rooting depths, final height, growth rate, and shade tolerance, they've been arranged to symbiotically contribute to each other's success. (The updated term for this type of gardening is called "poly-culture," but let's not get caught up in semantics.)

Many new companion gardeners are concerned about the space occupied by nasturtiums, zinnias, calendula, and

Grasshopper on a sunflower

other flowers, and note that the flowers decrease the space available for vegetables. Ultimately, in my experience with companion planting, I've found that an interplanted bed is often capable of producing a higher output of produce, even though flowers and herbs take up some of this space. Pests are distracted by the flowers and herbs, or eaten by beneficial insects. The edibles are left to thrive and grow much healthier and more robust than they would have otherwise.

I've included designs for a plethora of interplanting within the specific plant chapters of this book. However, if you've moved beyond the "beginner" level, and would like to try your hand at designing your own companion planted bed, make sure to take the following interplanting requirements into consideration. All of the following should be compatible in order for a companion planted bed to work as intended.

Growth Rate—I once made the mistake of seeding squash and nasturtiums in a companion planted bed on the same day. The squash had sprouted and started to produce vines before the nasturtiums had even developed a single leaf. The nasturtiums barely flowered all summer and were summarily devoured by the squash.

Companion plants don't have to have the same growth rate, but they can't swallow each other as they grow. Plants with a short final height and a long growing season can be planted with crops that grow upright and tall but not crops that grow outward.

For example, squash is known for its vining habit—it can take over an extremely large space by the season's end. Radishes also work well with squash beds. Seed radishes within the squash beds, and unlike nasturtiums, they will be ready for pulling before the squash requires the space. Corn also grows well with squash because of its upright shape, and it will linger through most of the season without being overwhelmed by squash vines.

Nasturtiums still have a place in my squash beds, but now I make sure to start the nasturtiums indoors to give them a head start on the season.

To avoid the same mistakes in your garden, evaluate the growth rate of any plant before adding the seed to the ground.

Crop	Approximate Days from Seed Until Harvest
Radishes	25 to 30
Broccoli, beets, cucumbers, greens, lettuce, spinach, turnips	45 to 60
Beans—bush and pole, cabbage, carrots, cauliflower, collard greens, peas	55 to 75
Melons, eggplants, peppers, sweet corn, tomatoes, watermelons	68 to 85
Brussels sprouts	80 to 90
Fennel, pumpkins, sweet potatoes, onions	100 to 110
Parsnips	120 to 130

Jerusalem artichokes at midsummer

Plant Nutrient Requirements	
Light feeders	Beets, carrots, garlic, horseradish, Jerusalem Artichokes, leeks, onions, potatoes, radishes, sweet potatoes, turnips, tomatillos
Moderate feeders	Brussels sprouts, cabbage, cauliflower, collards, kohlrabi, kale, lettuce/greens, parsley, spinach, Swiss chard
Heavy feeders	Artichokes, Broccoli, celery, corn, cucumbers, eggplant, garlic, melon, parsnips, peppers, pumpkins, squash, strawberries, tomatoes
Soil builders	Peas and beans and all other legumes

Nutrient Needs—While eggplants rely on rich soil to generate large fruit, lettuce will still grow in soil that has been depleted. Peas and beans add nutrients. Heavy feeders should be rotated with soil builders and light feeders to give the soil a chance to rebuild its supply of nutrients. If heavy feeders have occupied a bed for most of the growing season, spread a nutrient dense cover crop, like crimson clover, in the fall to replenish the soil.

Available Sunlight—Trees, fences, shrubs, and competing vegetables can all block sunlight from reaching the kitchen garden. Most vegetables prefer full sunlight, though some will tolerate partial shade. It makes sense to plant some crops within the shade of their sun loving companions. Keep track of the sun's path across your garden during the day. Our garden faces the south, so the tallest crops are planted in the back of the garden or towards the back of each bed.

Make sure to plan the garden according to a plant's final height at the end of the season. Jerusalem artichokes may start small, but they can reach up to 10 feet in height. They and other tall or trellised plants should occupy the space on the northern side of the edible beds.

Vining crops often perform better when they're trellised to grow upwards. Squash and cucumbers will grow naturally towards the sunlight they crave. Crops that prefer partial shade, like spinach and cucumbers, can occupy the space below.

Location—Even if you grow bushels of peppers, it's not a requirement that the plants must all share the same bed. If half the peppers appear in one section of the garden, and the other half in another, it leaves space for interplanting.

Because garlic is known for its protective and repellant smell, I plant it all over my garden. A few cloves are tucked into the perennial beds, others surround the fruit trees, a singular row graces two or three beds, and a few more have a small plot towards the front of one of my larger beds.

There is debate among companion planters about whether to plant crops of a similar variety in the same bed, or to spread them out. On one level, it makes sense to plant a bed of collards, broccoli, and kale because they're all brassicas. If one plant becomes infected by a fungus or infested with a pest, the devastation will be limited to that bed of the garden, and with crop rotation, it will die out the next year. However, by planting them in the same bed, it can encourage pests to make their approach.

I've found that it really depends on the type of crop being grown. If the crop is noted for its finicky nature and susceptibility to pests and disease, it really needs to be tended to in several smaller plots around the garden. But if a crop is hardy

Tomatoes and marigolds

by nature, it can occupy the same bed as some of its plant family members. In my garden, tomatoes are spread out among the garden beds, while kale, cabbage, and broccoli are grouped as family members.

Within the actual bed space, try to think beyond the idea of "rows." Rows certainly have a place in the garden, and some beds are configured best when crops are grown in rows. There is no requirement, however, that each crop grow in single file line down the bed. Let rows of crops mingle and weave between each other. In early spring, one bed might contain four tomato plants in a long singular line, peas scaling the face of the tomato cages, borage around the edges, and some chives at the southern corner.

Principle 3: Plant Intensively

When seeding vegetables and transplants in the ground, pay careful attention to their spacing. Mulch should be applied to the soil to surround the transplants while they are still small. Once the crops reach their final size, the "ground floor" of the garden bed should no longer be visible.

If one plant will be harvested before another in the same bed has even begun to produce, have an idea for the crop that will follow. A single bed might contain spinach and lettuce in the early spring, eggplants, peppers, and bush beans in

the summer, and then carrots in the fall. Gardeners often refer to this technique as succession planting.

The growing season can be extended with row covers, grow boxes, or cloches. Personally, I'm really fond of the hoop system devised by Johnny's Selected Seeds. They sell a Quick Hoops™ bender that can be used with galvanized electrical conduit, and two types of fabric to insulate crops for cold weather, or to act as a barrier to insects. I was able to bend the conduit myself with the hoop bender, and because the conduit is hollow, I could push them into the ground on my own also.

Principle 4: Flowers and Herbs Belong in the Edible Garden

It can be a trial in patience and faith to devote space in your garden to flowers and herbs. At first glance, flowers appear particularly superfluous. They might seem to be an aesthetic luxury—there to beautify the space, but not there to work towards your garden's success. I implore you to look closer.

The addition of flowers and herbs creates a more complex diversity of species. Biodiversity attracts beneficial insects, an army of allies who will aid you in your quest to keep garden pests at bay. An organic, companion planted garden hums with life—beetles, bees, and birds all visit, but most arrive as

---

About Chemicals

In my teaching career, there are some movies that I show each year to my seventh graders. One of those is the HBO biography *John Adams*, which we watch in bits and pieces during our discussion about the Revolutionary War. In one scene, the delegates are discussing whether they should declare independence from the British. The argument becomes quite heated, until one of the delegates flings his arms to the side and shouts "Not Now, Not Ever!" That pronouncement sums up how I feel about chemicals in the garden. If the whole purpose of your garden is to encourage life and growth, anything that has the suffix of "-cide" has no place.

friends, and not foes. Chapters 6 and 7 discuss some of my favorite annual and perennial flowers and herbs for the companion gardener. In Chapter 8, I explore the types of insects you might encounter in your garden.

Principle 5: A Companion Planted Garden Extends Beyond the Garden Border

All of the trees in your yard, your hedges, your perennial flower bed, the small creatures your garden shelters, and the weeds that grow nearby, should all be considered part of your garden's ecosystem. The trees and hedges harbor migrating and resident birds. Low growing vegetation creates a habitat for toads. In Chapter 6, I discuss how to create an inviting perennial bed, and how to attract friendly garden critters.

In summation, when preparing your companion planted beds, don't abandon the fundamentals of gardening; healthy garden soil is the literal and figurative foundation for any companion planted garden. Companion plants need water, sunlight, and loamy soil that is overflowing with microbial life.

An Eastern tiger swallowtail on a zinnia

Chapter 3

A GARDENING PRIMER

I always make time to just wander around my garden and observe my plants on a day-to-day basis. In fact in my classroom one day, one student mentioned my weird habit of "staring" at my garden. He told the class that he skateboarded by one afternoon, and I was just staring at the plants. When he traveled back home in the other direction, I still seemed to be just gazing around, albeit in a different location. He wasn't criticizing me, he just couldn't figure out what the heck I was doing!

Of course, he found this behavior odd, but I know it's crucial for my garden's survival. Those little observations I take in on a day-to-day basis provide me with the information I need to keep my garden healthy.

This is our outdoor cat Charlie in the garden. Charlie helps us hunt voles and mice, so her presence is welcome in the garden.

From observation, I can tell if my plants are thriving, and if I see any potential nutritional deficiencies, or evidence of disease, I can generally correct them before they become a big problem. I can also observe the rate at which my plants are growing, and their productivity level. I take time to notice what insects are visiting, and whether they are eating other insects, pollinating the flowers, or if they are munching holes in the plant leaves.

Close observation is important, and that's why I advocate it as your first step towards creating an abundantly successful companion planted garden.

Planning Your Garden

To make an organized plan for the year ahead, I'd suggest spending some time just observing the land you have available. Take a slow walk around your yard a couple times a week, for several weeks in a row, and jot down your observations. Here's a list of potential questions you might ask yourself as you wander.

• Where does the sunlight fall most frequently?

Most garden vegetables prefer full sun, so find an area in your yard that takes in at least seven hours of unfiltered daylight. Your garden does not have to fit in a rectangular or square shape. It's perfectly fine if the trees that shade your yard allow only for a triangular garden or some other uniquely curved configuration. In fact, while the confines of your available sunlight might seem restrictive at first, they might encourage a garden design that is more creative and visually appealing. If a tree does shade your entire backyard, you might want to reconsider how constructive it is for your gardening plans.

Once you've identified the pattern of sunlight in your yard, take some time to measure that space. Having these measurements on hand will give you some

parameters when you design your first garden beds.

Also, be aware of the slope of your yard and the way in which rain runs from the slope. If you live on a sloped plot of land, you will need to build some type of retaining wall to level the land. If the rain runs too furiously down the hill, it might be better to place your garden elsewhere.

• What creatures visit your yard presently?

This question also requires careful consideration. Visiting wildlife can be both beneficial and irritating to the kitchen gardener. While some aid the gardener by eating pests, others can ravage your vegetables and flowers. Take note of these critters as they can impact your garden plans. Watch for birds, rabbits, cats, deer, groundhogs, mice, voles, or any other animals that might visit. Larger visitors are best held back by a sturdy fence.

• What is the state of the land in your yard?

If you've newly acquired the land you live on, or recently decided to become a gardener, your land might presently be in a neglected state. Chemically treated lawns will require soil amendments for several years to return the soil to its natural level of organic microbial activity. Chapter 4 discusses how to identify the current composition of your soil, and how to improve the soil for planting.

Also, take note of any perennials that already exist in your yard. Try to identify the perennials specifically if you're not currently aware of their classification. Perennials play an essential role in any companion planted garden. Gardeners might identify some perennials as invasive weeds, but even those "weeds" often provide some benefit. Queen Anne's Lace, Goldenrod, and Joe-pye weed are allowed to grow freely on the edges of my yard. It's much easier to allow perennials to stay rather than rip them all out. Chapter 6 discusses the benefits of a perennial garden, and the types of wildflowers you should encourage around your garden space.

• What water sources are available on your plot of land?

Depending on the climate in your area of the country, free access to water will determine the type of plants you can grow and how many you can cultivate. Make sure the spot you pick for your garden provides you with ready access to a water source if you need to water in between rainfalls.

• What zone do you live in?

There are two numbers you should be aware of related to gardening.

Most plants have an ideal temperature range. The first number indicates the hardiness of your climate. You can find a specific number for your zone by visiting the following website: www.planthardiness.ars.usda.gov/PHZMWeb/. This number is often referred to as your "zone."

The second number is less known but has become increasingly important in recent years. In the 1990s, the American Horticultural Society developed a plant "heat zone" map. This map indicates the highest temperatures your climate will typically reach in a given year. This number is also crucial because most plants have a maximum heat tolerance. Spinach tends to set seed when temperatures reach the mid-eighties, the leaves of the lettuce plant turn bitter, peas stop producing new flowers—most plants have a breaking point.

You can see a miniature version of this map by visiting: www.ahs.org/gardening-resources/gardening-maps/heat-zone-map. To acquire more specific information, you can purchase your own printed copy.

Zinnias

While both numbers will provide you with the standard information for your climate zone, most people also have little pockets of exceptional shade or sun in the yard that create microclimates. In microclimates (as opposed to macroclimates), the conditions are slightly different from the yard as a whole. While your yard might have a general hardiness of zone 6, there might be a little patch on the southern side of the house, next to the front fence, that is actually closer to zone 7. The fence adds a windbreak and warmer shelter for tender vegetables. Microclimate zones can also be created when a wall or a fence creates a windbreak or when there's a marked difference in shade or sunlight. Some materials, like brick, absorb the sunlight during the day, and then release it at night.

I noticed a slightly warmer microclimate next to our garage. As fall made its seasonal approach and nightly temperatures became cooler, I observed which plants made it through each night. I knew my basil was susceptible to the cold, and in the main garden, it succumbed to frost in early September. Next to the garage, the basil lasted until early October.

After you've generated some answers to these questions and have begun to draw up plans for your garden plot, you need to think about the purpose behind your edible garden. What has specifically motivated you to grow on your own plot of land?

Maybe you've grown to distrust grocery store produce and would like to grow more healthful, seasonable alternatives. For me, my interest in growing my own vegetables was sparked after I ate my last sad, out-of-season, tasteless pale pink tomato. That spring, I had little cherry tomato plants set up on the porch of my apartment building.

If your goal is to save money on produce, it might guide your selection of plants. For instance, if you have limited space, homegrown tomatoes will save you much more money than onions. A bountiful bed of lettuce that can be clipped all season can provide the foundation for a simple salad a good portion of the year. If you've decided to plan your garden around calorie-rich foods, potatoes (sweet and regular), corn and beans might take up most of your space. A nutrient-rich garden might lead to beds full of kale, spinach, and carrots.

Maybe you've simply grown to despise mowing your lawn and would like to create an alternative landscape. With a smaller yard, a carefully planned garden might almost eliminate the need for a push mower.

Whatever your reasons, make sure you have them clear in your mind before you map your garden space.

Chapter 4

LAYING THE GROUNDWORK

Your soil is one of the key elements to cultivating a healthy companion planted garden. All the plants in your garden need healthy diverse soil from which to grow. If your plants are strong, they will be better at defending themselves against the hazards of the outside world—garden pests and disease. They will also attract more beneficial insects to the garden.

Once you've determined where you would like to place your garden, you should investigate the texture and the pH of the soil that is already present. There are two easy tests you can conduct to gain a greater understanding of your soil's composition and acidity level.

Test 1: Soil Composition

Soil is made up of three major components—sand, clay, and silt.

Sand drains well, but its nutrient level is exceptionally low. Sometimes sand drains too easily and can leave plants thirsty because it does not hold moisture.

Clay soil is much more nutrient dense, and it holds onto moisture greedily. Clay soil can suffocate the roots of plants by not providing them with adequate room to expand, and it is often unwilling to give up any of its water to the plants. If clay soil has not seen any rainfall for more than a few days, it will crack and split.

Silt is the best component of the three. Silty soil has characteristics of both sand and clay, but without the extremes. Silt can hold moisture, but it drains at a reasonable rate, and it generally remains aerated unless it's been compacted by extreme rains.

To determine the type of soil already present in your garden, you should conduct a simple soil test. Take a mason jar and fill it with about a cup of soil and a cup of filtered water. Shake the jar to thoroughly mix the soil and

D.I.Y. Soil Test

—— Silt
—— Clay

—— Sand

Test 2: A Soil's pH— Acid or Alkaline

I'd also recommend testing your soil's pH before planting. The pH of soil is measured on a scale between 0 and 14. A level of 7 means that your soil is neutral. Any numbers below 7 mean that your soil has some level of acidity. If your soil measures above the number 7, it means that your soil is more alkaline. Most vegetables prefer a soil that's slightly acidic— somewhere around 6.5.

You can have your soil tested by your local Cooperative Extension Service for free. Soil tests are also found at garden nurseries. You can also test your soil at home with a simple homemade test; however, a home test will not provide you with a specific pH.

To test your soil at home, take two mason jars and fill each of them with a cup of soil. Add some water to each to soak the soil. In the first jar, add a cup of vinegar, and in the second jar, add a cup of baking soda. One of the jars may bubble or fizz. If the vinegar jar shows bubbles, the soil is highly alkaline. If the baking soda jar fizzes, the soil is measurably acidic. If neither of the jars reveal any reaction, the soil is much more neutral.

If your soil does show some severe alkaline or acid levels, it should be amended with organic matter before adding plants to the soil. If the soil appears to have been relentlessly neglected over the course of several years, it might be better to devote a year to building the soil's tilth.

Unless your soil is markedly acidic or alkaline, you needn't be concerned. By gradually amending the soil with

the water. Then, set the jar on your counter to allow the soil components to settle overnight.

Once your soil has settled, you will see that it has divided itself into three layers. The bottom layer, with the grittiest particles, is sand. The middle layer is silt, and the top layer, with fine smooth particles, is clay. If all the layers are equal, your soil is of good quality. Soil with equal components is called loam.

If one component is greater than the others, your soil has more of that component. Having this knowledge can be of great help when you start to plant. While you won't be able to significantly modify the texture of your soil, by adding organic matter to the soil, you can overcome any deficiencies. Soil that is overwhelmingly sandy or clay based should be amended with aged mulch, compost, and cover crops for a season before the garden is even planted.

organic material, it will move towards neutral.

Life in the Soil

In order to take the steps necessary to feed your garden soil, you must first understand what healthy soil looks like on a biological level. Soil is alive and bustling with activity. The creatures in your soil—both those you can see, and those that are observable only on a microscopic level—wiggle through the dirt creating minutely sized pathways, eating and excreting as they travel.

The pathways aerate the soil and provide oxygen for the microorganisms to breathe. The aeration of the soil also encourages plant roots to grow uninhibited and provides tunnels for rain to settle. That rain absorbs into the soil and keeps it moist between rainfalls. You can feel this aeration in the soil by crumbling some through your hands. If your soil has a good amount of "tilth," it will crumble gently. Roots will grow in aerated soil unencumbered.

When the soil is compacted, there is nowhere for the rain to settle, no room for roots to spread, and no oxygen for microorganisms to breathe. Your plants' growth rate will be stunted, and the lack of oxygen will actually create a situation where toxic organisms can flourish.

Within the soil live macro and microorganisms. Macroorganisms are easier to identify because they're the organisms that you can see with the naked eye. If you take a moment to look, every time you stick your trowel into the soil you'll see an earthworm slithering back into a hole or a spider scrambling out of the way. Earthworms, spiders, burrowing insects, and burrowing animals, like voles and moles, all fit into the category of macroorganisms.

These macroorganisms break down fresh organic matter into small particles. Microorganisms—bacteria, algae, fungi, and many more microscopic microbes then feast upon the newly digestible matter.

As the microorganisms eat, digest, and excrete, they transform the nutrients in the soil, like potassium, calcium, and phosphorus, into a form that can be readily absorbed by the plant roots. This relationship between the organisms, the nutrients they release, and the plants that absorb those nutrients is the foundation for a garden that is full of life.

Improving Your Soil

In order to properly take care of the plants in your garden, you will also need to tend to the requirements of your soil. It is best to think of your soil as a living organism. Although the soil is actually composed of millions of macro and microorganisms—as they are all interdependent and interconnected, I like to think of it as a giant singular creature—friendly, generous, and hungry. This understanding helps me to frame how I should treat the soil.

Many gardening books used to suggest deeply digging garden beds at least once every season. The French method of gardening, the intensive method, or double-digging method, all involved exhausting amounts of labor in which the gardener would dig down deep into the garden beds and turn over soil each spring. In my first year as a gardener, I dutifully completed this process. My back hurt, and my arms ached, but my garden beds *appeared* to have fluffy aerated soil.

The concept behind this process was the understanding that by turning over the soil, compacted nutrients would come to the surface, and they would be more accessible to the plants. Also, the aeration created by the digging would allow roots to more easily penetrate the soil. Rototillers automated this process by allowing the gardener to plow through the garden bed, almost effortlessly turning the earth.

While these factors are both somewhat true, the same results can be achieved much more easily. You do not have to stress your back and exhaust your limbs to create healthy soil. Furthermore, deep digging destroys the ecosystem already present below the surface. It disrupts the delicate web of tunnels that have been knitted together by earthworms, insects, and microbes. Rototillers will slice through earthworms and annihilate your garden's workforce. The nutrients that arrive on the surface will be plentiful, but most will disappear before the plants absorb them. The digging process will also transfer the soil on the surface deep into the bed. As the top layer of soil is "dead," and without microbes, that dead soil will now mingle with the plant roots. Deep digging also brings long buried weed seeds to the surface, and once they are unearthed, they will happily germinate after their long dormancy. The soil's fluffiness hides its weak structure—it will compact with the first hard rain.

This very process creates conditions similar to those that appeared during the Dust Bowl era. Prairie soil was deeply dug, and during the first years, farmers grew astonishingly large, nutrient-rich plants. Then, those nutrients depleted, and the farmers were left with only dust.

I'm not sure why gardeners have chosen to replicate this process on a smaller scale, but obviously, it doesn't work. The gardener will only be burdened with large amounts of heavy lifting, and their soil will ultimately require heavy fertilizer and more frequent rototilling to continue a reasonable level of production.

Instead of employing such aggressive and laborious maintenance, it is better to construct a system where the garden's soil organisms generate healthy soil for you. Feed the soil with organic matter, like mulches and compost, and improve its structure with cover crops or soil amendments. The bacteria, fungi, nematodes, and insects consume the food and convert it to soil through decomposition. As I work with the natural cycle of the garden, I don't disturb the soil with aggressive tilling, and I don't kill it with chemical fertilizers.

Building Healthy Soil Naturally

Building healthy soil requires a combination of four elements, including compost, mulch, cover crops, and fertilizer.

Composting

Even if you only have the slightest space available for your garden, I'd suggest carving out a tiny portion for a compost pile. A compost pile is an essential piece of a companion planted garden. Compost replicates the natural process of decomposition and contributes to the sustainability of your garden beds by regenerating the previous season's waste into food for the next generation of plants. Because it's crafted by microbes from decaying plant matter, it naturally contains

all the minerals necessary for growth. It also retains more water per pound than clay or sand, and as a result, it reduces the need for continuous watering.

Before you start to build your compost pile, plan its placement. It should be easily accessible from the house and garden. If you live in a hot climate, pick a location in the shade. If you live in a cooler climate, pick a location in direct sunlight.

Cold Compost vs. Hot Compost

There are two main ways to generate your own compost—cold compost and hot compost. Building a cold compost pile requires little thought or planning. Leaves, grass clippings, garden and yard debris, kitchen scraps—all can be heaped on the pile without any concern for ratios, moisture levels, or heat. For those new to composting, a cold compost pile offers the simplest way to reduce waste. It's a location to toss organic materials from the kitchen and yard that doesn't involve a plastic bag or a garbage can.

Unfortunately, cold compost piles also come with several deficits. Cold compost can take up to a year to break down, and with such a slow rate of decomposition, it probably won't provide you with all of the compost you will need. If you don't bother to break up larger pieces of materials—like stems or branches, the process can take even longer. Cold compost also doesn't generate the heat needed to kill weed seeds or pests.

Fortunately, a hot compost pile isn't that much more challenging to build, and the quick production rate of usable compost can be oddly satisfying for the kitchen gardener.

Building a hot compost pile requires a greater attention and awareness of the process of decomposition. In order to speed up the aerobic activity in your compost pile, you will need to maintain even ratios of nitrogen (green materials) and carbon (brown materials). Green garden materials have a high moisture content, and brown compost materials are dry.

To build a hot compost pile, gradually layer green and brown materials until the pile is three to four feet tall. Each layer should measure approximately 6 inches in depth. If the materials are dry, water the pile as the layers are built. I always like to throw in a shovel or two of finished compost with each layer for an additional burst of microbial activity.

In drier climates, a compost pile can dry out if it has too much sun. Cover it with a tarp to hold in the moisture, and if needed, add some additional moisture with a hose. Ultimately, the pile should have the moisture equivalent of a damp sponge.

You can tell if your pile is heating up by giving it a quick turn with a pitchfork. Hot compost piles can reach up to 160 degrees Fahrenheit on the interior, and will visibly steam from the heat. You do not need to turn the pile every few days for the compost to work. Turning needlessly exposes nutrients to the atmosphere, and it's better to trap those nutrients on the interior of the pile.

It's imperative to maintain even levels of brown and green materials when creating hot compost. With too many green materials, the pile will turn anaerobic, and it will start to smell. The odor can be horrendous when a pile contains only green materials, and compost has garnered an unjust reputation because of this smell. A well-balanced compost pile will have no stench. If there are too many brown compost components in the pile, the materials won't deteriorate.

Materials for your Compost Pile

Nitrogen-Rich/Green Compost Materials

Grass clippings

Fresh plant materials

Manure/soiled animal bedding (Only include manure from herbivores and chickens. Horse manure can contain weed seeds, so it should only be included in hot compost piles.)

Cover crops (also known as green manures)

Kitchen scraps (leftover vegetables, coffee grounds, tea bags)

Crop debris (like brassica leaves, tomato leaves, or bean and squash vines)

Garden weeds (Hot compost piles can include weeds that have gone to seed. The hot temperatures will kill any seeds. If you'd like some extra security for placing them in the pile, let them slosh around in a plastic bin for a few weeks with some water. Once you've cultivated a nice blackish sludge, it can go on the pile.)

Carbon-Rich/Brown Compost Materials

Dried leaves (preferably chopped)

Straw

Wood shavings

Dried stems from spent plants

Nut shells

Sawdust (don't use dust from pressure treated wood, or plywood shavings)

Newspaper/office paper/cardboard—all can be added to the compost, but be careful about adding paper if it has colored ink.

This list is not meant to be exhaustive. I've composted wool scraps from my knitting, paper towel rolls, coffee grounds, and chicken feathers. You need to switch your mind towards composting instead of automatically reaching for the garbage can. Chances are, if the product in your hands was derived from natural materials, it can probably go in the compost.

If the materials are chopped more finely, they will turn to compost at a faster rate. Crumble leaves, shred newspaper, break down the materials into smaller portions as much as possible.

Once your compost looks like crumbly soil, and no longer includes the characteristics of elements that were tossed in the original pile, it's ready for use.

To avoid—Never add plants that have been infested with disease. Also, don't add bones, meats, or any oils. Manure from your dogs and cats should also be avoided. Dogs and cats are carnivores, so their stomachs (and excrement) contain worms that can be harmful to humans. Finally, glossy magazines and pressure treated wood contain toxic chemicals and shouldn't be composted.

Mulching

Creating mulch employs many of the same elements contained in compost. While mulch is also aged, it still retains much of its former appearance and texture.

By incorporating mulch made from organic matter into your garden, you can hold moisture in your garden beds and reduce the frequency of overhead watering. Organic mulch also fertilizes existing plants, aerates the garden beds, provides shelter for beneficial insects, and minimizes weed germination. When it rains, the soil won't compact, and the plants won't get that icky coating of mud sludge or sand. The nutrients in mulch will eventually become part of the garden as they are tilled lightly into the soil in the fall. The soil organisms will cheerfully munch away on their new food supply.

My plants seem happier and more content when they're surrounded by mulch, and the garden beds look neat and tidy. With an attractive mulch like chopped leaves, the focus turns towards the actual plants, the plant combinations, and not the soil below.

For a companion planted garden, I much prefer mulches derived from organic matter. Chopped leaves, grass clippings, pine needles, and newspaper are among my favorites, as they are all available for free, and they will ultimately disintegrate. Even if you have a small yard, and a minimally sized lawn, you can still find bags of leaves, grass clippings, or pine needles along the roadside in fall. I generally allow any debris intended for mulch to age for a few weeks in a pile along the side of the garden.

In the past I employed plastic as one of the mulches in my garden, but I've since avoided its use. Black plastic will warm the soil and kill weeds. Unfortunately, once it's exposed to the sun, it will deteriorate in quality, and it often becomes riddled with rips or tears. The now useless plastic will take a thousand years to disintegrate, and obviously, it offers no nutrients. My garden has been around much longer than myself, and from time to time, I dig up plastic that was laid down by the previous inhabitants.

To integrate mulch as part of your garden, wait until the soil has warmed in the early days of spring, but before the summer weeds have germinated. The soil should be relatively dry and not soaked from a spring rain or melting snow. Remove any overwintered weeds, and shovel an inch or two on the top of the bed. Make sure to add newspaper as the bottom layer if immediate weed germination is a concern. Mulch can also be integrated when seedlings are transferred to the outdoors. Leave a bit of space between the mulch and the seedlings to prevent the stems from rotting. Because I garden in a northern climate, I like to add mulch once in the spring, and again in the fall. If you live in a warmer climate, it might be better to add mulch more frequently, as the heat can make the mulch break down faster.

Mulch will moderate soil temperature, cool season crops like cabbage and broccoli can be kept cooler with a layer of mulch. For warm weather crops, like peppers and eggplants, don't apply the mulch until the soil is sufficiently warm.

Varieties of Mulch

Comfrey

The comfrey plant might seem misplaced in the mulch section, but I promise, I added it here for a good reason. Comfrey is a large leafy plant that blooms with pretty clusters of bell-shaped flowers. The roots of the comfrey plant reach deep down into the soil and supply the leaves of the comfrey plant with nitrogen, potassium, and phosphorus. After it becomes established the first year, comfrey will grow fast and furious. I cut the leaves back several times within the season and spread them at the base of my plants. Comfrey pairs better with plants that flower and fruit. It's been shown that placing the plant mulch around root crops can make the root crops flower before the tubers reach a substantial size.

Comfrey is native to the British Isles, and it's perennial in zones 3-9. Some varieties of comfrey will spread rather voraciously, so if space is an issue, try a sterile variety called "Blocking 14."

Grass Clippings

I love using grass clippings in my garden. They offer a fine mulch around plants sensitive to weed competition, like onions or garlic. They are chock full of nitrogen, so they can add a boost to the soil in nitrogen deficient areas. Also, although they can be tedious to spread in the garden bed, they will last the whole season long. Make sure to only use chemical free grass clippings as part of your garden. Also, don't include grass that has gone to seed. The seeds will quickly sprout, and you'd shortly have to combat a new generation of weeds. For best practice, leave grass clippings in a short pile until they brown before spreading them in the garden. (Don't make your pile too large all at once. I once left a large pile of grass clippings in a corner of my garden, and for weeks I was convinced a devious farter was hiding among my vegetable plants.)

Whole, Chopped, or Rotted Leaves

Wood leaves are best employed in the garden as a winter blanket over cold sensitive perennials. They can also be utilized to encapsulate crops towards the end of the growing season for a protective frost barrier.

Chopped leaves make a better midseason mulch. When chopped, the leaves are less susceptible to the wind, and they can be applied around young plants to prevent weed germination. At the end of the season, the leaves can be worked into the soil. They will break down during the winter season and amend the soil with fresh organic matter.

Chopped leaves can also be left in a pile to break down, and they will turn into a splendid soil amendment called leaf mold. Leaf mold retains water at an incredible rate, so it holds moisture in the soil. Chopped leaves will not transform into leaf mold quickly, it can actually take more than a year.

To make leaf mold, just pile chopped leaves into a corner of the yard. Turn the pile with a pitchfork every once in a while. When the leaves appear soft and fluffy, the leaf mold is ready for use.

Wood Chips, Bark, and Sawdust

Wood chips are best saved for garden pathways, or as mulch around trees and shrubs. Freshly decaying wood can be allelopathic, so it's better to let wood chips age for a few months if you've decided to incorporate them in your garden beds.

I've picked up bags of wood chips at a local sawmill for free. If you see a town tree removal service driving by, try asking them for their leftover wood chips. As they generally have to pay for wood chips removal, they will gladly drop a load of wood chips in your yard without charging you.

Avoid commercially dyed wood chips. The dye is a chemical, and it doesn't belong in your organic garden.

Bark chips can make an eye-catching ornamental mulch around perennials or shrubs, but they don't really belong in garden beds around vegetables. Bark chips are often applied in landscaping because they don't break down quickly. Unfortunately, they don't add any nutrients to the soil either.

Aged sawdust can be added as mulch to edible gardens, but it must be allowed to age before incorporation. Fresh sawdust is too high in carbon, and it may burn young plants. Like wood chips, sawdust is often available for free at the local sawmill.

Newspaper or Cardboard

Newspaper and cardboard are most commonly utilized as the bottom layer of sheet mulch. The dense nature of the material creates a thick barrier that prevents light from filtering through. Weeds will die, and new weeds won't germinate. It is best to think of both mulches only for their weed prevention possibilities. Neither holds much in the way of organic nutrients.

Pick newspaper pages with only black ink and rip off any plastic labels from cardboard boxes. While cardboard can be laid down in a single layer, newspaper should be added 10 to 12 sheets at a time to create a sufficiently thick layer.

To keep newspaper in place, add it to the garden on a calm windless day. Wet the sheets once they are laid down, and weigh them with additional layers of grass clippings, chopped leaves, or compost. Let the leaves break down over winter, and the bed can be planted in the spring. Even if the newspaper or cardboard you spread in the fall has failed to break down before planting time, you can still leave the layer in the garden bed. Poke suitably sized holes in the cardboard or newspaper, and place your plants within the holes.

Aged Manure

Technically speaking, you can add manure to your garden from any vegetarian animal. Before you shovel any manure into your compost pile, you need to scrutinize the source.

Some animals are fed with hay from fields that had previously been sprayed by broad-based herbicides that will survive in the digestive system of the animal, and then attack your garden. Other manures are generated by animals that have been fed antibiotics or deworming medication. Horse manure often contains hay seeds that will germinate if it is not composted properly. With all of these caveats taken into consideration, if you have a source for fresh manure that is free of any contaminants, definitely take on as much as you can for your compost.

Before any manure is laid on garden beds, it needs to age. Fresh manure contains too much nitrogen, and it can burn plants. Either add manure in the fall and give it the winter to age, or let it age in the compost pile for at least 6 months.

Pine Needles/Pine Straw

The needles break down quite slowly, so they make an appealing mulch in perennial beds and as a cover for beds in transition. They also can be utilized as a fine mulch around asparagus or strawberries in a perennial bed.

Even though pine needles are slightly acidic with a pH of 6.0 to 6.5, the needles will not increase your garden's soil acidity by any great margin.

Straw or Hay

Those new to gardening might be confused by the difference between straw and hay. Hay is meant for animal feed. It contains the seeds of whatever plant it came from (clover, alfalfa, wheat, etc.), so if spread in a garden bed, it will sprout a whole new generation of weeds.

Straw is the by-product of hay production and is primarily composed of the hollowed stalks of the cereal crop. It's safe to use in a garden because it shouldn't contain any weed seeds. Only use straw in garden beds if weed issues are minimal. Straw will allow some light through to the soil, and weed seeds can germinate. It is possible to try a double layer of mulch with newspaper, and straw. Some gardeners cover the beds in winter with straw for a layer of protection, but it also creates lovely accommodations for mice and voles.

Salt hay comes from the grasses that grow in salt marshes. It does have seeds, but without required elements of salt marsh soil, the seeds will never germinate. Salt hay (or cord grass) is often incorporated into the garden along the garden pathways. It can be expensive, so look to cheaper alternatives if you can't find an inexpensive supply.

White clover

Cover Crops

Cover crops are green manures that feed the microorganisms and earthworms in the soil by building organic matter. The microorganisms turn the organic matter into nutrients for the plants and improve the soil's tilth. They also increase the water absorbing capacity of the soil, aid in the construction of a soil web, and build biomass. They also prevent erosion.

Low growing cover crops like crimson clover or oats can be planted around existing plants to prevent weeds from germinating—this is why they're called "living mulch." As the name suggests, living mulches grow under edibles during the season, and they can then be gently cut down and tilled into the garden soil in the fall.

When the roots of cover crops shed, they will decay in the soil, and build organic matter deep underground without any of the disruption of a tiller. Their flowers can attract beneficial insects, and sometimes, they'll confuse or distract predators.

Some cover crops, like hairy vetch or field peas, aid in nitrogen fixing, and others are known as *dynamic nutrient accumulators*. Dynamic nutrient accumulators collect nutrients from deep in the soil. When their leaves shed, or their growth is chopped back, their decay builds nutrients on the surface level of the soil. Cover crops are often broadcast over an empty bed in the fall, and then tilled lightly under in the early spring. They can also be covered by fresh mulch or compost. Given a few weeks to decompose, the decaying crops will release nutrients in time for a new season of seedlings.

Other cover crops are best incorporated into the garden as a space holder between crop seasons. I find it best practice to never leave a bed completely empty of plants. Even if I don't get a chance to plant a new crop, I quickly broadcast some cover crop seeds over the soil. The cover crop will smother weeds before they can germinate, prevent soil compaction, and build up nutrients. When beds are cleared of debris and spent plants in the fall, cover crops will act as a placeholder until winter and the root structure they generate will prevent nutrients from leaching from the soil. Some cover crops, like hairy vetch, will shift into dormancy during the cold season, and then begin growth again once spring temperatures return. When new beds are added, cover crops can boost nutrient levels before the first edibles are sown.

Cover crops are absolutely the swiftest way to improve soil, and they belong in every garden bed at some point in the season. You really can't pick the "wrong" cover crop for your beds, but if this is your first season working with cover crops, start with a couple of variety packs. Add an option or two to your selection each year, and see what works best with your garden soil and your climate. I've included a list of some of my favorite cover crops below.

To plant a cover crop, broadcast the seeds lightly over the soil and till them approximately an inch below the surface. Don't over seed. In most cases, it's best to cut down the crop when the crop has just begun to flower, but before the flowers have bloomed or the crop has set seed. At that point, the crop will contain both nitrogen and carbon and will decompose quickly when tilled back into the soil. The crop will need warm soil to decompose, so it's best to incorporate the crop in mid-spring or in early fall. After digging it in, leave the crop for at least three weeks to decompose.

Varieties of Cover Crops:

Alfalfa—Perennial—*medicago sativa*

I mention alfalfa here because it's an extremely popular cover crop; however, I don't recommend it for kitchen gardeners. It has to grow in the same plot for a full year, and it's difficult to eliminate from the soil once it's established.

Buckwheat—Annual—*fagopyrum esculentum*

Buckwheat is a fast growing cover crop for use during the summer growing season or as a placeholder in garden beds. Plant at any point throughout the summer, and till it back into the soil before it sets seed for a green manure. Do let it flower sometimes, as its blossoms will attract hoverflies. With its quick growth, buckwheat is also excellent at smothering persistent weeds like quack grass. It won't survive frost.

Crimson Clover—Annual—*Trifolium incarnatum*

Crimson clover produces gorgeous red flowers that will entice beneficial insects. It prefers shade and cool seasons, so plant it around broccoli and Brussels sprouts and other brassicas for living mulch. It will often survive in the garden bed over winter in zones 6 and higher, and bloom in late spring. Crimson clover will also fix nitrogen, build the soil, and offer a foraging source for birds. Decaying clover is allelopathic, so till any decaying clover into the soil a month before planting any edibles. (Crimson clover is not the same crop as red clover.)

New Zealand White Clover—Perennial—*Trifolium repens*

White clover is often incorporated as living mulch under edible crops. This type of clover has a deep taproot (3') that works to aerate hard compacted soil. New Zealand white clover has demonstrated tolerance to drought and heat. It can also be planted as a cover crop in early spring or fall. The flowers will attract beneficial insects.

Field Peas—Annual—*Pisum sativum*

Field peas will fix nitrogen and grow readily in cooler weather. They're often found in a mixture with other cover crops. Field peas are most commonly planted in early spring and tilled into the soil to make way for warm weather crops. They are often sown with oats. The pea shoots are edible, so trim a few for your plate before you till them in.

Hairy/Winter Vetch—Annual—*Vicia villosa*

Hairy vetch is winter hardy and can overwinter even in northern climates. As a legume, it will fix nitrogen in the soil, especially if the seeds are inoculated prior to sowing. There is also scientific evidence that hairy vetch will promote disease resistance in vegetable crops. Plant hairy vetch in early fall to encourage its establishment before a hard frost. Hairy vetch is often companion planted with winter rye or oats. If hairy vetch is planted in the spring, allow the crop to deteriorate for 2 to 3 weeks before planting any edibles. The flowers of hairy vetch are a pretty purple, and they attract beneficials.

Oats—Annual—*Avena sativa*

A cover crop of oats should be sown in early fall. In northern climates (zones 6 and lower), the oats will die with the frost. They can then be quickly tilled in the spring. It's not necessary to wait the requisite month before planting because the oats have already died with the fall freeze. Oats can also be planted with fall broccoli or cauliflower, and then left in the plot once the plants are harvested. Oat seeds also germinate readily in cooler weather. If you decide to plant oats at an alterative point in the year, make sure to till the growth into the soil before seeds form.

Mustard—Annual—*Brassica juncea*

This cover crop is often grown to help control nematodes and harmful soil fungi. It's reputed to help with the growth of potatoes. If you let some of the crop set seed, the seed can then be harvested for some homegrown mustard. Mustard will die with the frost, so it's best planted in early fall.

Winter Rye—Perennial—*Secale cereale*

Winter rye grows rapidly, especially in mild weather. Spread it over soil early in spring before weed seeds have had the chance to germinate. The growth rate of winter rye will grow faster than the weeds and smother their development. As decaying winter rye can be allelopathic, wait a few weeks before planting anything new.

Winter rye is also often planted in fall, and it can overwinter in climates that reach well below zero. The trick is to plant in early fall so that the crop has a chance to become established before freezing temperatures arrive. The crop will become dormant during the winter, and then begin to grow again once spring arrives.

If you're new to cover crops, and have hesitated over which cover crops would be best to implement in your garden, consider purchasing a mixture instead. Johnny's Selected Seeds sells a *Spring Manure Mix* of hairy vetch, oats, and field peas. Territorial Seeds sells a *Fall Mix* of hairy vetch, crimson clover, Austrian field peas, and winter rye. Either will boost nitrogen levels in the soil.

Chickens are always willing to help break down compost.

Fertilizer

Fertilizer is designed to give a quick boost to plants during the growing season. All fertilizers are made up of some combination of the three required plant food elements—nitrogen (N), phosphorus (P), and potassium (K). Nitrogen boosts leaf production, potassium (sometimes called potash) promotes cell division in roots, and phosphorus helps plants form flowers, and then fruit. Of course, leafy plants like nitrogen heavy soil, and plants with large fruits or roots require greater amounts of potassium and phosphorus.

Every product you add to the garden soil also acts as a fertilizer. Green manures, wood chips, compost, and aged animal manure can all be considered fertilizer. If you add organic material to your garden each year, you will spend less and less time separately enhancing the soil with fertilizer.

All fertilizers are labeled with three numbers. The numbers represent the levels of nitrogen, phosphorus, and potassium. For example, if you find fish emulsion that is labeled 5-3-3, this means that the fertilizer contains 5 percent nitrogen, 3 percent phosphorus, and 3 percent potassium. Chemical fertilizers often showcase flashy numbers that reach much higher, but remember that any short-term gains will result in depleted soil in the long term.

Plants also need smaller amounts of minor nutrients, including calcium, magnesium, manganese, copper, and iron. If you work with exclusively organic fertilizers, they're more likely to possess some of these minerals instead of just fertilizer filler.

Not surprisingly, I utilize naturally derived fertilizers in my garden and avoid any chemical or synthetic sprays. Chemical fertilizers possess such an overwhelming amount of nutrients that the organisms in the soil will gorge themselves on the excess of nutrients, and then deplete the soil of carbon. The level of organic matter in your soil will actually drop, and then the soil organisms that are still left will turn to your growing plants for a food source.

Store bought natural fertilizers can often be expensive, so over the years I've started making a few of my own. I've included my recipes for comfrey tea, fish emulsion, bone meal, and aerated compost tea on the following pages.

Honestly, I don't obsess over fertilizer. I've piled on tons of organic material every year, so I know my plants and soil organisms are content. I use my DIY liquid fertilizers to give my plants a boost as they grow. I make bone meal because I like to return the chicken bones from my home raised chickens back to the earth.

Making Comfrey Tea (8-3-20; *This ratio refers to the comfrey concentrate. Dilute to 1/15 strength before pouring on soil or leaves.*)

Liquid fertilizers, like fish emulsion, or comfrey spray can be applied during the season, and the nutrients that they provide are readily accessed by growing plants.

To make comfrey tea, just harvest leaves from the comfrey plant, chop them up, and stuff them in a large 5-gallon plastic bucket with some water. The leaves will rot, decompose, and transform into a noxious sludge. The water can then be sprayed on plants with a spray bottle attached to the hose. I make sure to spray some directly on the leaves of any plant in the cucurbit family. A recent study in Russia indicated that comfrey tea might stop powdery mildew spores from germinating.

Making Fish Emulsion (5-3-3)

Fish emulsion is one of my favorite fertilizers for the garden. It costs me pen-

nies to make, and although it may be completely in my mind, I'm pretty sure I can literally see my plants perk up once they have been sprayed. I like making my own because it's economical and because I can cultivate a bucket full of microbial activity.

To make your own fish emulsion, add the following ingredients to a 5-gallon bucket:

- 3 to 4 shovels full of compost, aged manure, or an equal amount of well-aged leaf mold
- 1/2 of a cup of blackstrap molasses to aid fermentation
- 8-10 cups of fish scraps. I pick mine up from the fish market down the road. If you don't have a source for fresh fish scraps, you could also use canned anchovies or herring.

Stir all the ingredients in the bucket, and fill the bucket with water, leaving a couple of inches of room. Place a cover over the top to stop flies from laying eggs in your fish stew. I like to take a couple of pieces of burlap and tie them over the top with some twine. It dulls the smell and allows the brew to breathe. Don't cover the bucket with a plastic lid. The brew "grows" as it ferments, and the lid could explode from the top of the bucket if it's sealed too tightly.

Let the fish emulsion brew for a month or so. Remove the lid every few days, and give the bucket a stir. The smell is completely horrendous the first week, but it calms down with time. If you live in close proximity to your neighbors, you might want to warn them about your concoction in advance, or they're liable to think you've buried a dead body in your backyard when they catch a whiff downwind.

Once the fish emulsion is finished brewing, I strain the solids from the brew, and use a spray bottle attached to a hose to spray around the roots or on the leaves of garden edibles. I've read many articles that note the smell of fish emulsion, but I don't notice it too much when it's sprayed outdoors. I do have to wear gloves during the spray application. I sprayed one time without any gloves, and my hands reeked of dead fish smell for days.

Making Aerated Compost Tea

I first decided to make aerated compost tea after reading *Teaming with Microbes*. This book provides an excellent synopsis of the helpfulness of aerated compost tea in your garden. The following directions are derived from their book.

To brew your own aerated compost tea, you will need the following items. With the exception of the aquarium air pump and the air stone, you should be able to find the rest of these items around your house.

Necessary Materials
- 5-gallon bucket
- small bucket with a lid (for your compost)
- aquarium air pump
- air stone (to connect to the air pump)
- duct tape
- some type of porous bag (I just used pantyhose)
- 4 cups of compost
- molasses/maple syrup/fruit juice (for growing the microbes)
- fruit pulp (for growing the fungi)
- 4 tablespoons of oatmeal

Mix the compost and the oatmeal together. Add a small amount of moisture (it should look like a crumbled brownie).

Place the lid on the container, and move it into a warm dark place. After three days, it should have white mold growing over the top. This process encourages the growth of fungi in the aerated compost tea. If you don't see any fungi after three days, just let it sit a bit longer.

Once you have sufficient amounts of white fungi, put your compost inside the pantyhose, tie it in a knot, and place it in the 5-gallon bucket. Tape the air stone to the bottom of the bucket with duct tape, hook it up to the aquarium air pump, add water, and plug it in. Make sure your tea brews away from direct sun.

Wait 24 to 36 hours. While the compost is aerating, you can add the molasses and fruit pulp to help aid in the growth of microbes and fungi. Your tea should smell like earth. If it doesn't, your compost has turned bad, and should be tossed.

The tea should be used shortly after brewing.

The aeration process brews bacteria, fungi, nematodes, and protozoa that can then be transferred to your garden over and over. These organisms will improve the soil food web in your garden soil and will help defeat the pathogens and diseases. The bubbling of the compost in water creates an aerobic compost tea.

Making Bone Meal (1-11-0)

Some of you might read this section and wonder about my relative sanity. I probably don't need to do this with the animal bones from my kitchen, but I find it difficult to throw any available organic matter in the trash. We raise our own chickens for meat, and I make chicken stock with the bones. A few years ago, when the chicken stock had been drained from the pot, I was left with a clean pile of chicken bones. Some gardeners bury the bones directly in the compost heap, but we live in a somewhat rural area, and I was concerned that the bones might attract carnivorous animals. I decided to try my hand at making bone meal.

To make your own bone meal, you can use any kind of animal bones, so long as they can fit in your oven. When I make chicken stock, the bones are boiled for a day or so, so the bones are fairly clean once they're removed from the pot. If needed, clean the bones of any remaining soft tissue.

I then heat the oven to 400 degrees, and bake the bones until they're dried and brittle. To transform the bones into bone meal, they need to be broken down into crumbles. Some gardeners use a high-powered food processer, and others use a mortar and pestle. My technique is slightly less delicate. I like to throw them all into a bag (like an empty dog food bag), and pound them with a hammer until they've broken down. I'll spread the bone meal on the garden in the fall. The rest of the year, I turn the meal into the compost.

Building the Beds

Now that you're aware of all the major elements that combine to create healthy garden soil without tilling, it's time to build some new garden beds.

My garden is planted almost exclusively in raised beds. Raised beds make it possible to plant much more intensively than a traditionally rowed garden. It's estimated that if you transform your long, singularly planted space into a garden with raised beds, you can grow five times the amount of garden produce. I've noticed a dramatic upswing in the amount of produce I've harvested once I made the transition.

Wide beds reduce the space allotted to pathways and permanently delineate between pathways and garden soil. As a result, gardeners are no longer confronted with the yearly issues associated with soil compaction. The soil in the garden beds is never compressed, and any disruption from footsteps is minimized. I've also found that permanent beds create a more conducive structure for companion planting and crop rotation. When the width of the bed measures 4 or 5 feet, instead of 1 or 2, it enables a diversity of plants.

Lining your beds with a border is not required, but the borders create a permanency of structure. Also, logistically speaking, when the borders of a garden bed are built with greater height, it's easier to pile on the organic matter, as the borders demarcate a container for your layers of sheet mulch.

I built my beds from available materials. Most are lined with old bricks, and I also built a few with cedar planks. Some are raised only a few inches from the ground, and others are about a foot tall. I've seen beds lined by concrete blocks, sections of a log, long limbs of trees, straw bales, and stone pavers. Really, you just need a material that can establish some type of border. My first beds were built with materials that could be adjusted as I contemplated the garden's redesign each year. Permaculture enthusiasts advocate beds built with curved lines, and I've found that curved borders give me the space necessary to wield a wheelbarrow around the garden pathways.

To construct your first beds in the garden or to build additional beds, you can and should, employ a technique known as sheet mulching. If you've ever made the effort to rip up sod to start a new section of garden, well, you've made too

much of an effort. Removing sod is tiresome, and it can take hours to clear a slight section of your yard. It also exposes long buried weed seeds to sunlight, and without consistent maintenance, that newly cleared piece of land will be filled with weeds within weeks.

Instead, I much prefer to sheet mulch new garden spaces. Sheet mulch is much, much faster! If the necessary materials are close at hand, an entire garden space can be sheet mulched in the time it would take to rip up sod for a singular garden bed. Sheet mulch also lays the foundation for nutrient and microbial rich garden soil.

With sheet mulch, the lowest layer of a bed should be made up of a dense material that can block light, usually newspaper or corrugated cardboard. The blocking of light is crucial to stop weed germination. Whenever I lay down the cardboard or newsprint, I spray the layer with some water to keep it from blowing away with the wind.

At this point, I prefer to pile the coarsest materials next, and with each layer, the materials should be finer in texture. Near the top I add a layer of compost, and then the pile is finished off with shredded leaves, straw, or pine needles—whatever I have on hand. Each layer is sprayed with water until damp. Ultimately, the pile should measure at least two feet in height—though the pile can reach 3 or 4 feet.

Each gardener has his or her own preferred technique for sheet mulching. Some swear by a German mulching technique called Hugelkultur (HOO-gul-culture), which involves a layer of decaying wood, branches, or logs at the bottom of the bed. Others make sure to add manure. Really, the order and density of each layer can be variable as long as some attention is paid to the ratio of green and brown materials. The sheet-mulched beds need a bit of nitrogen to jumpstart the microbial activity.

The best point in the year to construct new beds is fall. Microorganisms and earthworms have the chance to move in and encourage decomposition, and fresh ingredients like grass clippings and manure will have an opportunity to age.

Still, I recognize that most of you probably turn your eyes towards the garden in early spring. Thankfully, it's always possible to sheet mulch a garden bed, even on short notice. A thick lay of compost on the top of a sheet-mulched pile is suitable for small plant starts even when more coarse materials have just been laid. If your compost is in short supply, dig pockets of compost into the mulched bed, and add your transplants there.

Chapter 5

STARTING FROM SEED

Why I Start from Seed

I made the decision to start most of my plants from seed when I realized how limited the offerings were at my local big box store or even at the farmer's market. I also became concerned about the diseases that might be introduced to my garden by plants grown in unknown conditions.

Plants purchased at big box stores may have been treated with chemicals, including insecticides, fungicides, herbicides, and synthetic fertilizers, and there is no requirement that those chemicals be labeled. The plants are often carted from a giant industrialized farm to the store, often in close quarters. Most likely, they are not cared for with the same individualized attention that I can devote to my seedlings.

At my local farmer's market, the conditions are much improved, but the plant varieties offered are still limited. For instance, at my local market, there are undoubtedly 10 or 12 options if I'd like to buy a tomato plant. Product offerings are based on popular will, and tomatoes are a popular choice among those with small gardens. Some of the plants at the market might even come from organic seed, and they were probably grown in a healthy climate. I can even consult with the farmer who grew the tomato plant to find out if they were grown organically.

But, I also love broccoli. I love to grow broccoli in the spring and again in the fall. In the spring, if I venture to the farmer's market to find broccoli plants, there's a 90 percent chance that I'll only find one kind.

Fewer gardeners grow broccoli, and as a result, the selection is more limited.

In midsummer, the only broccoli plants I'd find at a nursery would likely be hold-overs from the spring, shriveled and root bound, and not likely to produce any actual broccoli. Broccoli seedlings are also rare at farmer's markets in midsummer. In this case, if I'd like fall broccoli, starting my own seedlings is my only real option.

I also have a taste for more unique crops. Tatsoi, collards, Brussels sprouts, and Mache, among many others, have all been grown in my garden at some point, and all must be started by seed if I wish to have them there. Heirloom plants are also difficult to find locally, and I like to experiment with new heirloom seeds every year.

Also, I direct seed many of my short season flowers and vegetables straight into the garden. In my 5a climate, zucchini, radishes, squash, beans, zinnias, and peas all grow easily from seed during the summer growing season. Crops with a long taproot, like carrots or parsnips, should also be seeded directly in the garden. Those of you who garden in warmer climates have even more options.

By raising my plants from seed, I'm able to save space in the garden for more mature plants. I thin the weaker seedlings

---

Purchasing Plants

If you're making plans for your first garden ever, or if you find yourself with limiting time constraints, don't be turned away from gardening by the idea that you must grow your entire garden from seed. It is possible to purchase quality plants if you follow a few guidelines.

1. **Buy your plants from a reputable local nursery or direct from a farm stand at the farmer's market**. If needed, talk with the proprietor to make sure that the plants haven't been treated with any chemicals or grown with synthetic fertilizers. (Obviously, this point is not required, but as I strive for a chemically free garden, it is one of my considerations when I make a purchase.)

2. **Examine the plants to make sure they are healthy**. Check to see that they are not root bound, not diseased, and that they are not inhabited by pests. (I once bought a few plants from a local farm stand that came with a free set of squash bugs. Even local farmers might accidently sell infested plants, so be careful.) Healthy plants will exhibit a deep green hue and a stocky central stem.

3. **Consider how much produce you will yield from each plant you purchase.** I always laugh to myself when I see little four packs of onion seedlings. Sometimes a four pack of onion seedlings might only contain twelve onions. Make sure your plant choices are cost effective.

early on, so only the strongest survive to the point of transplant.

Finally, the most obvious reason for starting my own seeds is that it saves me money. If I were to purchase all of the plants I include in my garden, I would save much less on the produce they generate.

Ordering Seeds

All of this measured reasoning ultimately led me to the glory of the seed catalog. I often start the New Year with a mug of hot coffee and a pile of seed catalogs to peruse. For a newer gardener, seed catalogs can be quite overwhelming. Even I have to make a clear list, and stick to a budget. To make this process less daunting, I've provided a step-by-step guide to seed ordering for a companion planted garden. If you've gardened before, you might find it unnecessary to follow every step. Because I love gardening, my nerdiness for the subject means that I dutifully follow this process each year. Also, because I'm a teacher, I've always been a big fan of list making. (I like writing lists, drawing a line through items on the list, making tangential lists—you get the idea.)

Review Your Seed Supply: Some seeds can last up to five years, while others will only germinate for one. Most seeds are marked with the year they were originally packed. Cull any seeds that are unlikely to germinate. Additionally, if you didn't like the taste, yield, or growth rate of a particular variety, don't grow it again! Don't waste space in your garden for plants that are just so-so.

Garlic chive seeds

Seed Longevity	
Years Viable	**Crop**
1 year	Leeks, onions, parsley, parsnips
2 years	Corn, peppers, spinach
3 years	Arugula, beans, broccoli, carrots, peas
4 years	Beets, Brussels sprouts, cabbage, cauliflower, celery, celeriac, Swiss chard, eggplant, kale, kohlrabi, mustard, pumpkins, summer squash, tomatoes, watermelons, winter squash
5 years	Artichokes, collards, cucumbers, lettuce, melons, radishes, turnips

Make a List: If this is your first year gardening, brainstorm a list of the vegetables you'd like to grow. Don't be specific with varieties at this point. Just make a general list of possibilities. As much as it can be extremely difficult in January, when you're just dreaming about the potential, try to be realistic. If you've gardened in previous years, think carefully about what you'd prefer to grow again.

Possibly you were really jealous of your friend's gorgeous cantaloupes, and you'd like to try some of your own. Maybe you didn't grow enough spinach, or you've recognized that you don't really need piles upon piles of cucumbers. My seed list has changed over the years as I decided to grow more vegetables that I could store without canning. Squash and sweet potatoes have taken over some of the garden space that used to grow tomatoes or peppers.

Choose Your Plant Beds: In the plant-by-plant section of this book, I've provided a multitude of companion plant bed options. Use the list of vegetables you've generated to pick the best plant combinations for your garden.

Notice that I've provided notations that describe how your plant beds might change throughout the growing season. Obviously, unless you're considering an expansion, plan for the beds that you already have in your garden, not the garden you're dreaming about for the future. In Chapter 9, I discuss garden journaling and design. I would suggest mapping out the garden beds for the year before finalizing your seed order.

Revise and Finalize: Now, based on your plant bed selection, you can revise your growing list. You might be able to add in some vegetables I suggested as plant combinations, or you might need to remove some if you don't have the space. You also might add a list of flowers and herb seeds you'd like to pair with your vegetables.

Look back through your seed packets. Obviously, if you have enough seeds for the coming growing season, you can cross off those vegetables, herbs, and flowers from your list.

Order Your Seeds: I've included a list of reputable seeds companies I trust in the back of the book on page 249. Don't feel the need to acquire every seed catalog possible. In my first years as a gardener, I just ordered from one or two. Some vegetables have hundreds of varieties. I've made suggestions for each of the most popular plants in their respective chapters later in the book.

Be careful when reading the descriptions included in the catalogs. A bean might be described as "prolific" and "reliable," but if the catalog writers have failed to mention its taste, it may be

horribly bland. The catalog writers often play up a crop's best assets, so read attentively.

In your garden catalog, you will see labels that designate the type of seed you're purchasing.

Hybrid—These seeds are the product of decades of crossbreeding. Select seed varieties are painstakingly crossbred to promote admirable traits, like disease or pest resistance. They may also exhibit greater yields and grow with more vitality. The seeds from hybrid plants are not "true seed," and they cannot be saved. Hybrid seeds are often labeled as "F-1." Because of the breeding required, these seeds are often more expensive than heirlooms.

Open Pollinated—Open pollinated seeds are more consistent genetically. Seeds collected from these plants will produce offspring with the same traits, as long as the plants are isolated to prevent cross-pollination. Some plants require only a few yards of isolation for true seed, while others will only prove true if a mile or more separates similar varieties. These seeds will have adapted to the climate in which they were raised, so it might benefit to order from a seed company that has a similar climate to your own.

Heirloom—Just like the heirlooms of a family, heirloom seeds have a fun backstory. Seeds may have been passed down from generation to generation. Maybe only an Uncle Leonard in Wichita grew them over 25 years, maybe they are tied to a small town in Ohio, or maybe they are of a particular strain that was propa-gated by Thomas Jefferson. Some possess an extremely unique color, flavor, or texture. Heirloom seeds should have at least 50 years of specific identity. Whatever the story, all heirlooms are open pollinated. Not all open pollinated seeds are heirlooms.

Many gardeners have become concerned about the use of GMO (Genetic Modified Organisms) crops and seeds. Thankfully, as of right now, no GMO seeds are sold to individual gardeners. However, the main company that produces GMO seeds (Monsanto) also produces a good portion of the seeds sold to individual gardeners.

Starting Your Seeds

You won't need to start a good portion of your seeds indoors. Much of your garden produce will grow from seed to harvest in the garden bed. Determine the date of the average last spring frost in your region, and count backwards using the chart below. Don't let overeagerness cause you to start your seeds too early. A plant can become root bound if it spends too much of its life in a small pot. Plants that are root bound will actually take

Sowing Timetable for Indoor Seedings	
12 to 14 weeks	Chives, leeks, onions, celery, celeriac
8 to 12 weeks	Artichokes, lettuce (the first succession)
6 to 8 weeks	Calendulas, eggplants, peppers, tomatillos, tomatoes
5 to 6 weeks	Basil, Brussels sprouts, cabbage, beets, broccoli, cauliflower, kale, kohlrabi, lettuce (second succession), nasturtiums, spinach, Swiss chard Marigolds—Marigolds bloom about 8 weeks after germination. You may wish to start them indoors so that they're more mature (and protective) when they're planted in the garden, but they can also be seeded outdoors. Zinnias—Zinnias only germinate after soil temperatures have reached at least 75 degrees. Start seeds indoors if you like to have early season blooms.
2 to 4 weeks	Cucumbers, melons, pumpkins, squash—For gardeners in zone 5 or higher, these seeds can easily be started outdoors. Start indoors if you'd like to get a jumpstart on the season, or to avoid late season pests or disease.

The number of weeks listed refers to the number of weeks before the last frost date. Count backwards from your frost date to find the week that you should sow your seeds.

longer to grow in the garden, so any time gained by starting them early is lost once they reach the garden bed.

If this is the first year you've decided to start your seeds indoors, start small. Seed starting indoors does take some patience and time. By starting with only one or two trays, you can decide whether you'd find it worth your time to expand into a full-scale operation. Indoor seed starting also requires you to have an area of your home that will not be disturbed by small creatures (ahem—cats) who might take an opportunity to eat the tiny plants when they've been left alone.

To start your seeds indoors, you will most likely need at least one or two seed trays, some source of supplemental lighting, potting mix, plant labels and possibly a seed-heating mat. (Most seeds can sprout from a random cup with a bit of potting mix, but the trick is keeping them alive, and making it worth the effort to start them ahead of the season.)

If you live in a more temperate climate, the seeds can be started outside on a nursery table. As long as the table obtains at least 6 hours of sunlight a day, you won't need any supplemental lighting, and you might not need a seed heating mat. Lucky you!

Seed Trays: I've found that plastic seed trays offer the most versatility in seed starting and retain water the best. I've had mine for years, so I've reconciled the use of plastic with the fact that they're reused year after year. Initially, I started with trays that held 72 tiny seed cells. Over the years, I began to recognize that some seeds performed better if they were started in larger seed cells from the beginning. I now start my brassicas and my cucurbits in larger pods.

If you can't find any seed starting trays at your local nursery, Johnny's Selected Seeds offer seed trays with an assortment of sizing options. In addition, some seeds, like onions and leeks, merely require a quick broadcast over a bed of potting soil. They won't need individual seed cells.

If you'd like to avoid plastic altogether, soil blocks are another possibility. Soil blocks are aptly named as they are small blocks of soil that have been formed

with a small soil compressor. They will hold together without plastic cells, and the roots will not become root bound. Instead, they simply stop growing once they reach the edge of the soil block. The soil blocks can be contained in wood frames, so no plastic is used. Many large scale farmers use soil blocks, but forming perfect little soil blocks requires a bit of a learning curve. I'd hold off investing in one until you've decided that your gardening habit is going to stick.

Seed Heating Mat: Seed heating mats provide a gentle level of warm heat to help seeds germinate. Plants that grow best in warm weather conditions also have seeds that like a bit of warmth to germinate.

Lighting: Seedlings like close bright light. Unless the light from a nearby window is quite intense, you will need some type of hanging light to suspend over the seed tray. Seedlings will grow leggy and weak if they need to grow towards a light source. Seed catalogs often offer fancy lighting setups that are specifically devoted to starting seeds; however, I've found that any hanging shop light will work just as well. Also, shop lights are generally hung from adjustable chains, so the lights can be raised or lowered as needed. I've purchased ones that measure the same length as my seed trays, so there is no wasted light. If you only purchase one shop light your first year, you can still fit two seed trays under the light by switching them every twelve hours. The lights should be hung no more than 3 inches above the sprouts.

Potting Mix: You can buy premade potting mix for your seed starts, but I've found it's cheaper to make my own.

In a big bin, I mix equal parts coconut coir with vermiculate or perlite. I used to use peat moss instead of the coconut

coir, but once I read about the unsustainability of peat moss, I found that I couldn't really justify planting with a nonrenewable resource. Then I add in a layer of earthworm castings. The castings make up about 10-15 percent of the mixture as a whole. Sometimes I'll also add in some compost that I sift with a screen to remove any large particles.

Plant Labels: There should be a label for every plant cell you fill with soil and seed. I've made the misstep of only labeling "sections" of seedlings, and once the seedlings were transplanted, I lost track of the specific variety.

Starting Seeds Indoors

Before you plant seeds in your filled trays, premoisten the soil by gently pouring in some warm water. Let the water soak into the mix for a day. The potting mix should appear spongy but not soaked before you're ready to plant.

Seedling packets will provide specific directions regarding seedling planting. If you've collected your own seeds, remember the seeds should be planted about the depth of their width. This might seem obvious, but don't plant more than you need. Different varieties can be planted in the same flat, but they should have comparable rates of growth and condition requirements.

Seedlings should be kept consistently moist and never left to dry out completely. There is a real difference between moist soil and wet soil. The soil should never appear completely saturated. Potting mix does not hold water well, so the seedlings will need watering on a daily basis. I use a little water bottle spritzer as the seeds emerge. Directly pouring water into the cell packs can cause the seeds to uproot. Don't

overwater, and monitor for any algae growth, or signs of "dampening off." I'll also add a really small amount of an organic liquid fertilizer (like liquid kelp) to my spray bottle every two weeks. (Dampening off occurs when a small whitish mold growth appears on the soil surface.)

If you have one, place a seed-heating mat under the trays until most of the seedlings have arisen from

Transplanted seedlings hardening off on the porch

the soil. As they pop up, you will need to place them under some supplemental lighting. At this point, the seed-heating mat is no longer necessary. The lights need to be set close to the seedlings, no more than a few inches from the leaves.

As the seedlings grow and develop strength, gently brush the tops with your hands. The light touch of your hands is enough to stimulate root growth. You can also set a fan at the far corner of the room to generate a consistent light breeze.

Once the little shoots emerge, you will need to thin them down so that only one or two remain in each cell. Cut the extra seedlings with a small pair of scissors so that roots are not disturbed.

As the seedlings grow in size, some will need to be repotted in a larger container before they are planted in the garden. The process of repotting can encourage more rapid growth. Over the years, I've found it most valuable to re-pot my tomatoes, peppers, and sometimes my brassicas.

Transplanting

When transferring the seedlings to the outdoors, the plants will need some "hardening off." The term hardening off refers to the process of exposing the plants to outdoor conditions until they become acclimated to the wind and the sunlight. Don't rush this process. I've burned too many seedlings because I didn't adequately prepare them for the outdoor climate.

Plants should be set in a shady area of the yard and moved to a sunny spot late in the day. Each day, the plants can be transferred to direct sunlight an hour ear-

Transplanting day

Grow boxes can also be utilized for hardening off

lier. At first, the plants should be brought inside overnight. Gradually, the time they spend outdoors can be lengthened.

If possible, instead of having all your seed trays indoors throughout spring, allow some of the cooler weather crops to germinate outside. They will grow hardier and won't take as much time to harden off once warmer weather makes an appearance.

When pulling a plant from a container, pay careful attention to the roots and avoid disturbing their growth. If the roots have grown into a knot and become root bound, it's essential to loosen them from the ball. Otherwise, the roots will continue to wrap towards each other, and it will stunt the plant's growth.

Each seedling should have moist soil before transplant. Once the transplants are in the ground, water the seedlings and the surrounding soil.

Starting Seeds in the Garden

Some edibles prefer to spend the whole of their natural lives in the garden bed without the trauma associated with transplant. Crops that grow rapidly, like lettuce, spinach, and radishes, can all be started outdoors. Root crops that have a singular taproot, like carrots and parsnips, also prefer to germinate in the garden bed. Peas and beans also germinate effortlessly in the outdoor garden.

Chapter 6

FLOWERS FOR THE GARDEN

For a companion planting gardener, the process of creating a symbiotic, organic garden extends beyond the typical garden fence.

Planting a perennial garden that surrounds the vegetable garden on one or two sides introduces numerous benefits. The careful arrangement of perennial flowers to allow for continuous bloom will attract beneficial insects. Butterflies and other beneficial insects can find shelter from the wind in the perennial garden. The height and form of a perennial bed generates a shelter for wildlife and a protective wind barrier for the edible garden. Garden helpers like frogs, toads, and lizards will aid in controlling the pests by eating generous helpings of insects on a daily basis.

By adding in a few shrubs, or possibly a small tree or two, birds will take up a close residence. Birds are often described as garden pests, though I consider this description a bit unfair. Birds will poke at berries, and eat seeds, but if they're given better choices, they will often leave your crops alone. Some birds are pollinators and others eat pests. Look for robins, blackbirds, hummingbirds, wrens and sparrows—all serve a unique purpose. Shrubs give birds a place to perch and quick coverage from predators overhead.

Some pests actually follow the breeze, and the perennial garden acts as an obstruction to, or a distraction from, the main garden. Additionally, beneficial insects will switch between the perennial bed and the main garden as the pest population ebbs and flows. Most beneficial insects eat nectar and pollen along with aphids, caterpillars, and larvae. When the pests have subsided in the vegetable garden, the beneficials will wait for their return by taking up residence in the perennial bed or hedgerow.

Perhaps the best part of a perennial bed is that it makes a dramatic statement without requiring ridiculous amounts of upkeep. Perennials grow without the strenuous maintenance of an annual garden bed. Once the bed is established, it will only need a bit of attention each year to continue fruit-

Eastern carpenter bee on salvia plant

ful production. Unless there is extremely dry weather, perennials won't need much watering either. Perennials don't require tilling or seed starting, and fertilizing is necessary only once or twice a year.

Finally, the perennial bed offers some extra space to nurture the gardener. For those of you who argue that you could never have too many kinds of carrots seeded, or too much mulch—for those of you who gaze over your seed catalog with visible glee and delight, and for those of you always looking for the chance to snip a sly cutting—you must look to the perennial bed. If you find yourself drawn to the accumulative nature of gardening, the perennial garden provides the perfect outlet for your plant hoarding tendencies.

My perennial garden gives me the perfect opportunity to support my plant collecting habit. If I see a new shrub, flower, or bulb I'd like to try, I justify my "must have" attitude with the understanding that if I have a greater variety of plants, I'll further expand the biodiversity in my little ecosystem of a backyard. I'll also have less to mow!

Perennial Bed Guidelines

A little bit of planning will give you less work in the long run. Although I do spend some time increasing the size of my perennial garden, I don't really feel as though I spend much of my time "working" in my perennial beds.

On Location

There is a field across the road from our house, and the wind generally blows in from the field towards the garden. I purposely chose the location for the main perennial bed in front of the edible garden, and I created a wind barrier as a result.

If you have limited space in your yard, you can devote a bed in your vegetable garden to perennials, or you can plant a few perennials within your edible garden beds. Avoid plants touted as "fast spreading" for the edible garden beds, or they will soon take over any competing vegetation.

Bug bath

One of the many toads I've spotted in my garden.

A+ Accommodations

To attract and keep insects, frogs, toads, and birds in your yard, you need to construct an environment where they will feel safe, and one that will provide them with shelter and food.

Frogs and toads like to take up residence among the undergrowth of garden beds. We've supported their presence by setting up simple toad homes from clay pots propped up on stones. I've lost track of the number of times I've encountered a little toad when cleaning up garden refuse. With brown and gray colored skin, they blend in with garden soil effortlessly, so be aware of their possible presence.

To keep the beneficial insects around, add some bug baths to your edible and perennial garden beds. Bug baths can be made from ceramic or clay dishes. Just add some larger stones and a bit of water, and within a few days, the bugs will make a habit of stopping by for a cooling drink.

If a wooded area surrounds your house, birds will be attracted to the perennial garden with a simple birdbath. Birds also appreciate access to fresh water year round, so if you live in a climate with frost, add a warmer to your birdbath for fresh water in winter. As you expand your perennial garden, think about building a small pond or a heated water feature.

For those of you who live without many trees, you might consider adapting a section of your lawn into a hedgerow. In addition to a perennial garden, a hedgerow also includes bushes, shrubs, and small trees. You can build a hedgerow along the roadside, at the edge of the woods, or in the middling part of your lawn.

If the size of your yard doesn't include room for a generously sized hedgerow or a heated pond, at least include a few bird feeders, a small birdbath, and some perches near the garden space. Add some suet at the colder point of the year. Birds eat bugs, seeds, berries, and nuts—give them as many choices as your garden space allows.

During the winter months, leave some perennial foliage for winter shelter. Some harbor beneficial insect eggs, or the insects themselves. I'm especially skilled at letting dead brush, leaves, and foliage linger about in the garden after the fall season.

Start with Natives, remember Exotics, avoid Invasives

Our perennial garden has a mix of native and exotic plant species. I started building the garden a few years ago with a small planting of wild red Columbine and a generous patch of Bee Balm. New England Asters and some evergreens made up the center. A neglected mountain laurel shrub was transplanted from a shady spot in the back of the yard to a prime position next to the birdbath. Several native asters were added the next spring, along with a small Jacob's Ladder plant, and some Black-eyed Susan Daises. Tulips line the pathway next to the birdbath, and Camas bulbs and garlic cloves were planted this past fall.

As you can see, we allow both natives and exotics. Native plants attract native beneficials, and exotic plants attract exotic beneficials. While bulbs like tulips, daffodils, and crocuses are exotic, I love them because they bloom really early in spring, coax the honeybees from the hive, and present the bees with their first fresh food after a long winter. I collect native asters and varieties of bee balm because they are literally surrounded by insects every moment they're in bloom. I also try to pick plants that have many differently shaped blooms. Flies enjoy large clusters of blooms, like dill, yarrow, or asters. Bees are attracted to deep-set flowers where the sweeter nectar is hidden inside.

I let a few wildflowers survive in the perennial beds also. Many beneficial insects are first attracted to the beds by wildflowers like Queen Anne's Lace, Joe-pye weed, and Goldenrod—flowers with tiny, abundant blooms.

As you add plants to your perennial garden, have an awareness of when those plants bloom. Plant nurseries often stock plants that are in bloom at that moment. If you only plant in springtime, you might have created only a spring blooming garden. With each season, a new flush of blossoms should appear in your perennial beds, and hopefully, some flowers bloom all summer long. Extend this reasoning beyond blooming flowers, and try to think about how you will shelter birds and insects in each of the seasons of the year. Evergreens, shrubs, fruiting bushes, low growing ground cover, and vining plants should all have a place.

The only plants you should absolutely avoid are invasive species. Invasive plants will take over and dominate your perennial beds once planted. Often times, invasive plants generate an abundance of seeds that are then transferred unwittingly by birds or the wind, so you can't really keep them within the boundaries of your yard. Other species grow aggressively through their roots, and will literally smother any roots within their grasp. They will intrude on the growing space of their neighbors and are almost impossible to eliminate once they're established.

Unfortunately, awareness regarding invasive plants is still not where it should be, and I often spot invasive species at local nurseries. To find an accurate list of invasive species for your area, visit www.invasivespeciesinfo.gov/unitedstates/state.shtml.

I've generated a list of annual and perennial flowers I suggest for your companion planted gardens and perennial beds. There are thousands of beautiful flowers you can plant in your garden, and I encourage you to plant as much as your garden space allows. With this list, I focused on those flowers that were known for attracting pollinators and beneficial insects, those that are often paired with edibles, and those that are native to North America. I also discuss some of the possible uses for these flowers beyond the garden. I really want you to see your flowers as useful and not just pretty.

Some of these flowers work better within the garden, and others are best planted with perennials.

Columbine with asparagus ferns

Annual Flowers

Black-eyed Susans—*Rudbeckia hirta*

Black-eyed Susan flowers bloom in summer with daisy-shaped, bright yellow petals and dark brown centers. The plants reach 2 to 3 feet tall, and they grow and self seed without hesitation. These flowers fit well among edible garden beds, and the blooms will attract hoverflies, tachinid flies and parasitic wasps. They are native to North America.

Borage/Starflower—*Borago officinalis*

As an edible flower, borage is often classified as an herb. I think it blooms with delicate star-shaped blue flowers that make it too pretty for an herb classification. The plants reach over 2 feet in height, and can spread up to 3 feet in width. The leaves are greenish gray in tone. The seeds can be sown outdoors or given a head start indoors for early season blooms. If allowed to set seed, borage will self-sow, but it is not invasive.

Borage flowers attract honeybees and bumblebees and are reputed to support the health of tomatoes and squash and deter tomato hornworms. It is often planted with strawberries, and I've found it can help keep weeds in check in the strawberry bed. Borage is native to Eastern Europe (Syria).

Here, perennials surround a small water feature. Toads and frogs will make their home in the shelter on the low growing shrubs.

Here you can see nasturtiums, chamomile, and calendula intermingling.

Borage flowers make a colorful addition to salads, and the flowers can also be frozen in ice cube trays and added to a pitcher of lemonade. They have a light cucumber flavor.

Cornflower/Bachelor's Buttons—
Centaurea cyanus

Cornflowers bloom from late spring to summer with periwinkle-hued flowers an inch in diameter. The plants can reach approximately 2 feet tall and will sprout from seed without hesitation. Cornflowers are native to Europe, and they used to be a common wildflower there, but herbicides have reduced their habitat to the point where they are now endangered. Their early season blooms sustain honeybees and other beneficials.

Calendula (sometimes called Pot Marigold)—*Calendula officinalis*

Calendulas are lovely bright yellow and orange flowers that grow between 1 foot and 2 feet tall. They're native to Europe, so insects in the United States aren't really drawn to their aroma. The scent of calendula does seem to repel pests, so I include them with edibles in the main garden beds. A scientific study has shown that calendula can repel diamondback moths from cabbage (and possibly other brassicas). In another study, it was shown that their roots could revive chemically contaminated soil.

While I start my calendula inside to give them a head start, they will effortlessly sprout up when they are seeded outdoors, and they will often self-sow. The flowers favor full sun and respond well to repeated cuttings throughout the

Borage

Calendula with sage

summer. Calendula flowers are often confused with marigolds, and their names are incorrectly used interchangeably. Calendula is well known for its medicinal properties, so save and dry the petals for use in salves and soaps.

Candytuft (Annual)—*Iberis umbellata*

Candytuft flowers are low growing annuals with clusters of blossoms in pink, purple, and white (there are also perennial versions of candytuft). They will reach 6 to 10 inches in height. Their growth habit creates a habitat for ground beetles, and their blossoms attract hoverflies. Candytuft prefers full sun, and makes a perfect edging to a perennial garden bed, or as a border for salad greens or chard. It's native to Europe.

Calliopsis—*Coreopsis tinctoria*

Calliopsis is a daisy-shaped flower with yellow outer petals, and an inner red circle. This plant reaches 1 to 2 feet tall. If you deadhead the flowers, the blooms will last until frost, and they often reappear the year after. It's native to the North American plains, but it has spread throughout the rest of North America. It attracts butterflies.

Cleome—*Cleome hasslerana*

Cleomes are unique flowers with a singular stem and multiple tiny pink and purple flowers. They germinate readily and bloom from midsummer to early fall. They will reach a height of 3 to 5 feet, and their stems can become leggy and yellowed. They belong at the back of a flowerbed with other flowers to camouflage them at the base. Cleomes

will self-seed from year to year and are native to South America.

Cosmos—*Cosmos bipinnatus*

Cosmos can grow up to 6 feet in height and bloom with bright pink, white, and red flowers with yellow centers. Their foliage is feathery, lacy, and light. Cosmos actually favor soil that's sandy and not nutrient dense. They will generously sprout from seed, and once they bloom, they will bloom until frost. Their blooms are attractive, and they attract hoverflies, lacewings, parasitic wasps, and pirate bugs. If you're a neglectful or busy gardener, cosmos will be your steady friend. If you get the chance, pinch the stems while the plants are small, and the cosmos will grow into a bushy shape. Cosmos will readily self-seed in the garden if allowed. Cosmos are native to Mexico, Florida, and the southwest of the United States.

Geraniums (Annual)—*Pelargonium domesticum* (Perennial above zone 7 with protection)

Commonly known as scented geraniums, the leaves of these plants can smell like mint, roses, lemon, apple, orange, or chocolate. These plants are better known for the scent of their leaves, and they have less developed flowers. The plants generally reach 2 to 3 feet in height.

Traditional companion planters noted its ability to repel Japanese beetles, and their observations have recently been supported by scientific research. When Japanese beetles eat geranium flowers, they will become paralyzed for approximately 24 hours. While in this state of helplessness, predatory insects take the opportunity to attack. This research

Cleome

was conducted on the *Pelargonium* geraniums and not the hardy variety. Geraniums have also been reputed to repel cabbageworm and corn earworms. They are native to South Africa.

The leaves can also be dried and made into potpourri or steeped for tea.

Love-in-a-Mist—*Nigella damascene*

Love-in-a-Mist flowers bloom in colors of white, pink, and cool purples from spring to fall. They only reach 15 inches in height, so they fit perfectly under cauliflower, broccoli or on the edges of many garden beds. They're native to Southern Europe and North Africa.

Marigolds—*Tagetes patula* (French)

Marigolds are the flower most often cited in a companion planted gardening book. Even gardeners who don't consider themselves companion planters will often add marigolds to their vegetable plot. I like to interplant my peppers and

A yellow nasturtium

eggplants with marigolds. The musky scent of the marigold flower protects eggplants from flea beetle bites. Decaying marigolds can be allelopathic to brassicas and legumes, so I remove the plants from the garden at the end of the season and add them to the compost pile.

The allelopathic qualities of marigolds can also have pest-fighting capabilities. If root knot nematodes have taken over a garden bed, broadcast French marigold seed thickly over the entire plot, and turn them under at the end of the season. The root knot nematodes will enter the roots of the marigold plants and die.

Marigolds bloom from spring until fall with flowers of orange, gold, rust, and red. They will form into miniature shrubs 2 to 3 feet tall. They attract beneficial wasps and flies, and are native to the Southwestern United States and Mexico. They do not need any fertilizer.

Nasturtiums—*Tropaeolum* (Perennial above zone 9)

Nasturtiums are a unique aesthetic in the garden. They have rounded leaves and bright trumpet-like flowers that most commonly appear in shades of orange and yellow. They prefer semi-neglected soil, so they're a perfect starter plant for a new gardener whose soil still needs some improvement. Some varieties will send out cascading runners while others will grow into a low growing bushy shape.

Nasturtiums belong in a companion planted garden because they are beloved by aphids and will act as a "trap crop." Aphids prefer nasturtiums to most other plants and will jump to any nasturtiums planted nearby. The aroma of nasturtiums can also confuse pests, and their flowers will attract hummingbirds.

Nasturtium flowers are also edible—try them as an accent to a summer salad, or immerse them in a vinaigrette. They pack a peppery punch to your palate.

Sunflowers—*Helianthus annuus*

Although tall looming yellow sunflowers are the most recognized variety, sunflowers can actually range from 2 feet to 10 feet tall. The blooms range from 6 to 12 inches across, and attract hoverflies, bees, lacewings,

Orange nasturtium with rosemary

Zinnias

Propagating Plants

Many herbs and flowers can be easily propagated from stem cuttings. If you have friends who grow herbs, propagation is a really effortless way to add to your collection without added expense. You can fill a bed with the trimmings from five or six plants. Propagating through cuttings is an example of asexual reproduction. The new plant generated from the cutting will be a clone of its parent. Therefore, when making cuttings, choose those plants that are thriving in the garden beds.

To propagate new plants from cuttings you have collected, follow these simple steps:

1. Fill some small plant containers with potting soil.
2. Poke holes into each container with a dibble or pencil (skip if using clay pots as pictured.)
3. Cut some stems from an established plant. Each cutting should be around 5 inches in length.
4. Remove the leaves from the lower portion of the cutting. New roots will grow from the nodes of the cut leaves.
5. Dip the bottom portion of the cutting in some rooting hormone. (You can buy rooting hormone, or if you have access to willow branches, or raw honey, you can make your own.)
6. Insert the cutting in the soil, and press the soil surrounding the cutting to ensure stability.
7. Move the newly planted cuttings to a shady location. The cuttings should remain well watered, so they will thrive until they establish new roots. You can cover the cuttings with a plastic dome to maintain humidity levels if you wish.

and parasitic wasps. The seeds they produce will attract birds.

Sunflowers were traditionally planted with corn, squash, and beans as a "fourth sister" on the edges of a "three sisters" bed. Scientific studies have shown that they exhibit a measured level of allelopathy. In order to stake out their own territory, sunflowers emit a chemical that discourages seed germination and the growth of plant competitors. It's best not to grow them directly in the vegetable garden beds. Instead, add a row on the edge of a garden as a wind block, or add a strip of seeds to the perennial bed. Sunflowers are native to North America.

Sweet Alyssum—*Lobularia maritima*

Sweet alyssum is a low growing annual with a plethora of tiny blooms in white, pinks, and purples. The growth will reach only 8 inches tall, so the plants work best as edging, or in between walkway spaces. The blooms will fade after a few weeks, so give the flowers a quick trim to promote continued growth.

Sweet asylum creates a shelter for ground beetles and spiders and attracts hoverflies and parasitic wasps. It's native to Southern Europe.

Zinnia—*Zinnia elegans*

Zinnias are extremely simple to grow, and they will produce blooms from summer until frost. There are zinnias of almost every color, and while some reach only a foot in height, others grow to a height of 4 feet. The blooms attract a multitude of insects, including wasps, hoverflies, butterflies and bees. Because they are native to Mexico, zinnias prefer full sun—they will still produce with some partial shade.

Asters

Perennial Flowers

The Mint Family—*Lamiaceae*

Anise Hyssop—*Agastache foeniculum*—Perennial (zones 4–9)

Anise hyssop sports spikes of purple and blue flowers that attract butterflies, native bees, and hummingbirds and reaches 3 to 6 feet in height. It blooms in mid-summer.

Broadcast hyssop seeds in a section of the perennial bed to start your own plot. Anise hyssop flowers taste and smell like the anise herb, but anise hyssop actually belongs to the mint family. It's native to most of northern America, particularly the Great Plains.

Bee Balm/Wild Bergamot—*Monarda*—Perennial (zones 4–8)

Bee balm has a deliciously sweet scent that attracts all kinds of beneficials, including scores of honeybees, hoverflies, butterflies, and hummingbirds. It grows up to 4 feet tall, and it blooms in midsummer with spiky flowers in various shades of pink, red, and lilac. As a member of the mint family, it will spread beyond its original borders within several seasons, so pick a place where it has room to spread. Bee balm is native to the eastern coastline of the United States. It grows best in full sunlight and is susceptible to powdery mildew where there is too much moisture or shade.

Mountain Mint—*Pycnanthemum spp.*—Perennial (zones 4-8)

Mountain mint is one of the "must haves" in my perennial garden. It attracts so many pollinators, I had to move it away from the front of my house so they could feed without any disruption. I've seen bees, wasps, and hoverflies crowd the blossoms. The plants reach 4 feet in height, and they bloom with white flowers in midsummer. The leaves hold a spectacular "mint-like" smell that they release when brushed. As part of the mint family, the plant can spread, but it can be chopped back if it overgrows its allotted space.

There are several species of mountain mint, and each is native to a section of North America.

Tips for Procuring Cheap Perennials

Purchasing perennials can be expensive. Ask friends if they have any plants that need dividing. Offer to come over and help divide them up. Look for perennial plant sales in the springtime. Counties usually have spring garden sales, and the plants are reasonably priced. Also, I've often seen neighbors who have small perennials potted for sale.

The Aster Family—*Asteraceae*

Boltonia/Thousand Flowered Aster—*Boltonia asteroids*—Perennial (zones 4–8)

If you're just starting your perennial garden, Boltonia is one of those surefire plants that will grow faithfully without much care or attention. White daisy-shaped flowers with yellow centers bloom from August to October and they attract butterflies. This plant is native to most of the United States.

Coneflowers—*Echinacea spp.*—Perennial (zones 3–8)

Coneflowers are giant-sized daisy-like blooms with centers that measure at least an inch in diameter. The petals are often pinkish purple, and each bloom will reach approximately 3 feet tall.

Coneflowers grow from seed, but the roots can also be divided to generate new plants. Coneflowers are native to eastern North America. They attract beneficial wasps, flies, and praying mantis.

Cup Plant—*Silphium perfoliatum*—Perennial (zones 3–9)

The cup plant is so named because the flowers form a cup with their petals. They collect water and attract birds. The plants reach 3 to 6 feet in height, and they can spread quickly, so only plant if you have a generous space. It's native to most of the United States, and its blooms attract native and exotic bees.

Helen's Flower/Sneezeweed—*Helenium*—Perennial (zones 3–8)

Helen's Flower has small daisy-like blooms in colors that range from mahogany to a buttery yellow. The plant will reach 3 to 5 feet, and it often attracts bees. Helen's Flower unfairly earned the moniker "sneezeweed" because it blooms at the same time as ragweed. It's native to the eastern and southern portion of the United States.

Golden Marguerite—*Anthemis tinctoria*—Perennial (zones 3–7)

The plants reach 2 to 3 feet and bloom with bright yellow flowers. The blossoms attract ladybugs, tachinid flies, hoverflies, parasitic wasps, and lacewings. They don't require much care and grow well in poorly tended soil. This flower is native to Europe.

Goldenrod—Solidago—*Perennial* (zones 4-9)

Goldenrod is a beautiful wild flower that blooms in midsummer with tall (up to 6 feet), large tufts of tiny yellow flowers. It doesn't belong in the garden because it will quickly spread beyond its borders. Let a few sprigs pop up in the perennial bed to attract pirate bugs, wasps, bees, and hoverflies. It's native to North America.

Joe-pye Weed—*Entrochium fistulosum*—Perennial (zones 3–10)

Joe-pye weed can grow up to 7 feet tall or more depending upon the condition of the soil. It has large flower heads with a multitude of small lilac florets. It belongs at the center of a large perennial bed or towards the back of a garden. The flowers attract thousands of pollinators and birds love the seeds. It's native to the eastern half of the United States.

Tansy—*Tanacetum vulgare*—Perennial (zones 3–9)

Tansy is a large feathery plant with yellow button flowers that bloom in midsummer. It is held with high regard among companion planters because it's able to attract a multitude of beneficial insects to the garden, and its fern-like leaves are reputed to repel ants.

Unfortunately, tansy is considered an *invasive species* in many parts of the country. It can spread through underground rhizomes and through its seeds. If you decide to grow tansy in containers, chop it back in the fall before its flowers turn to seed heads. It is toxic (thujone), so don't plant in a location where any animals might have an opportunity to graze (most grazing animals don't like the taste anyway). It also has a level of toxicity for humans so avoid consuming it in great quantities.

Tansy was traditionally regarded as a culinary herb; it was brought to the colonies from Europe for that purpose and

Honeybee on Joe-pye weed

cultivated for a long period in American gardens. Seeds inevitably invaded roadsides, fields, and it spread throughout the country.

Yarrow—*Achillea millefolium*—Perennial (zones 3–9)

Yarrow is a feathery plant with clusters of tiny yellow or white flowers. It can reach 3 feet in height. Yarrow will self-seed in the garden readily and doesn't require much attention. The small clustered flowers of yarrow attract all kinds of beneficial insects, including hoverflies, ladybugs, and parasitic wasps. It can be included in the garden and pairs well with cucumbers. It's originally from Europe, but it has naturalized in North America.

Others:

False Indigo/Blue Wild Indigo—*Baptisia australis*—Perennial (zones 3–10)

False indigo blooms with tall spikes of pea-shaped blue flowers in mid-spring. The plant will then generate brown seedpods that will last for the rest of the season. The plant ultimately measures 3 to 4 feet in height and width and it favors full sun or partial shade. Its flowers attract butterflies, parasitic wasps, and lacewings. False indigo is native to central and eastern North America.

The plant is called "false" indigo because it was used as a blue dye replacement in the colonial era.

Queen Anne's Lace

Nodding Onion—*Allium cernuum*—
Perennial (zones 2–9)

The nodding onion blooms with a striking round cluster of purple flowers. The plants reach 10 to 12 inches, and flowers attract native butterflies. Plant it along the border of a perennial garden. It's native to the Pacific Northwest.

Sea Pinks/Sea Thrift—*Armeria maritime*—
Perennial (zones 4–8)

Sea pinks are low growing flowers that bloom in colors of white or pink. They reach only 1 foot in height, so they belong along the border of the perennial garden. They're not native to North America and were originally found in the northwestern part of Europe.

Queen Anne's Lace—*Daucus carota*—
Perennial (zones 4–9)

Queen Anne's Lace is a biennial flower that blooms with incredibly detailed white flower clusters. A member of the carrot family, the taproot of the plant is actually edible and tastes really sweet. The plant reaches up to 4 feet, and the white flowers attract ladybugs, hoverflies, parasitic wasps and lacewings. The flowers are found throughout North America, but it is not originally a native plant. It can crowd out other natives in the perennial garden, so only let a few sprouts survive each year.

This list only discusses a few of the available flowers for your perennial garden. To find flowers native to your area, visit wildflower.org. This website allows you to search through a database of 7,000 wildflowers. You can narrow your search by name, plant family, habitat, and state to find plants best suited for your perennial patch.

Don't limit yourself to the flowers I've mentioned specifically. Snapdragons and celosia are both beautiful. If you have flowers you love, don't feel that you have to get rid of them just to companion plant.

Chapter 7

HERBS FOR THE GARDEN

Herbs are indispensable in my companion planted garden. They act as living mulch for edibles, they attract beneficial insects, and they can deter pests by masking the scent of vegetables. They also find their way into most of the dishes we cook, into soap, medicinal remedies, and even the water we drink. We'll brew a pitcher of cold tea with fresh grown herbs in the summer, and warm tea is often drunk in the afternoon during winter.

As an avid herb collector, I add a few new herb varieties to my garden each year. I always mark each new addition with a secure plant label for reference. For a quick and easy crop rotation of perennial herbs, plant some in pots that can follow their plant companions from bed to bed.

When purchasing herb seeds or plants, try to check the Latin name to verify you have the correct plant. Herb names often overlap, and their common names can generate some confusion for the newer gardener.

> **Herbs for Propagation**
> Anise
> Basil
> Caraway
> Catnip
> Catmint
> German Chamomile
> Chervil
> Lavender
> Lemon Balm
> Lovage
> Oregano
> Rosemary
> Sage
> Southernwood
> Spearmint
> Summer & Winter Savory
> French Tarragon
> Thyme
> Sweet Marjoram

Anise—*Pimpinella anisum*—Annual

Anise blooms in early summer and will eventually grow to about a foot and a half tall. It blooms with small white flowers in small clusters, similar to Queen Anne's Lace. It provides a host for many beneficial insects, including lady beetles and tachinid flies. Although it is an annual, it can self-sow for successive seasons. Plant it around vegetables that bloom. Anise seeds have a licorice-like taste and can be used to flavor cookies.

Dark opal basil and Genovese basil

Basil—*Ocimum basilicum*—Annual

Generally speaking, basil grows best in warmer weather, and most varieties grow to 2 feet in height. There are several dozen varieties of basil, including brightly flavored lemon basil, cinnamon basil, and a purple Thai basil. *Genovese* basil is more popular among gardeners, and my particular favorite as it can be turned into a delicious pesto. Basil plants pair well with members of the nightshade family, along with cucumbers and asparagus. Companion gardeners have noted that it can improve the flavor of tomatoes. Leaves can be pinched from the plant throughout the summer. Make sure to cut directly from the first main shoot early on so that plant develops into a bushy shape.

Caraway—*Carum carvi*—Annual

Caraway is a good herb for the perennial bed. It will self seed readily, and it attracts a multitude of beneficial insects. Also a member of the carrot family, it blooms in spring with clusters of small white flowers. The seeds of caraway taste like licorice. It adds lovely flavor to winter soups and stews and is often utilized in canning. To capture the seeds for your herb collection, hang the seed heads above a tray, and let them fall at will.

Catnip—*Nepeta cataria*—Perennial (zones 3–9)

Catnip is known to attract beneficials like bees and parasitic wasps, and it is reputed to repel pests. It will bloom in the later part of summer with tiny pink flowers, and it can grow to 3 feet in height. Catnip can be invasive and allopathic to other plants, so its best place is in the perennial garden in a container. It also is quite intoxicating to cats, and they will eat the stems down to the nub. If your area is inhabited with outdoor cats, it might be better to avoid catnip in the garden. If you do decide to plant it, collect the leaves to provide a treat for your (indoor) cat, or you can make some tea for yourself. Catnip also repels mosquitos, so you could include a potted plant of catnip on your back porch.

Catmint—*Nepeta faassenii*—Perennial (zones 4–8)

Although it bears the moniker of "mint," catmint does not possess the spreading habit of other mints. Bushes will grow to 3 feet in diameter. Catmint grows well in poor soil, so it's an easy addition to a newly created perennial bed. While cats will not eat catmint, they do love the aroma, and they can often be found lying among the leaves.

German Chamomile—*Matricaria recutita*—Annual

German Chamomile grows 3 feet tall, and it will bloom throughout the summer with tiny white daisy-like flowers that attract bees. In the garden, it can be included as a cover crop around brassicas or peppers. Sometimes German Chamomile is confused with Roman Chamomile. Both have little white flowers and a similar aroma, but Roman Chamomile is a perennial, and it grows low to the ground. Like creeping thyme, it can be used between stones in a path or as a border to a bed. With both varieties, you can pick and dry the flowers for tea, or the flowers can be steeped with oatmeal for a calming bath.

Cutting celery and chamomile

Chervil—*Anthriscus cerefolium*—Annual

Chervil grows well in the shade and will seed best if it's planted directly outdoors in spring. Because of its shade preference, it pairs well with taller plants, like tomatoes. It can also be planted with greens as it shares similar growing requirements. Another member of the carrot family, it also produces clusters of small white flowers, and it will attract beneficials. It will eventually grow to around 2 feet in height. It possesses an anise flavor like parsley, and it can be used in place of parsley in a dish.

Chives—*Allium schoenoprasum*—Perennial (zones 3–9)

Chives have quite the positive reputation in the world of companion planting. They are known for their repelling properties and are often planted among the edible beds to repel aphids and Japanese beetles. Gardening lore suggests that planting them with carrots and tomatoes improves the edible's flavor. They are one of the first herbs to make an appearance in my garden in the spring, and they are a welcome addition in the kitchen when my onion stores have dried up. Chives grow in clusters of tall stems with purple blossoms and can reach a height of 2 feet.

Chives have the distinction of being the only member of the allium family to be found in both the "old" world and the "new" world. They can be added fresh to dishes for an onion-like flavor, or the stems can be chopped and dried. The flowers can be added to salads as a garnish, and I've infused them with white vinegar for pretty pink-hued vinegar. I also grow garlic chives (*Allium tuberosum*), and I've noticed that they hold similar repellant qualities. To multiply your quantity of chives, divide established plantings each spring.

Cilantro/Coriander—*Coriandrum sativum*—Annual

Cilantro and Coriander as often confused, and with good reason—they're both

Cilantro, chives, and basil

Dill flowers and anise hyssop

the same plant. When the seeds first germinate, the leaves they produce are cilantro. Once the weather warms, and the plant bolts, the seeds it generates are called coriander. Its tendency to bolt easily can prove annoying to the cilantro lover, but the flowers it generates attract ladybugs, hoverflies, parasitic wasps and lacewings. To some palates, cilantro tastes like soap, so conduct a quick taste test before you add it to any dish. Coriander seeds can also be collected for use in the kitchen.

Dill—*Anethum graveolens*—Annual

Dill is a graceful, tall, wispy plant with feather-like foliage. Dill will bolt with prolonged warm weather and produce heads of tiny green flowers that attract beneficial insects. It can grow to three feet before it bolts, and after bolting, it can reach 6 feet. It will self-sow easily, so let it set seed. It pairs particularly well with brassicas because it can attract beneficial wasps. In turn, the wasps will attack cabbageworms and cabbage loopers. It can also be planted with lettuce, onions, and cucumbers. Dill also provides a habitat for beautiful green and black caterpillars that will transform into swallowtail butterflies.

Fennel—*Foeniculum vulgare*—Perennial (zones 5–10)

The fennel herb plant has wispy feather-like leaves, and tiny clusters of yellow flowers that will attract a multitude of beneficial insects. It bears a sweet licorice taste that permeates its leaves, stalks, and seeds. *Bronze* fennel can grow up to 6 feet tall, and *green* fennel generally reaches 4 feet.

Some varieties of fennel, called Florence Fennel, will also grow a large bulb at the base that can also be harvested and eaten. To avoid cross-pollination, fennel should not be grown near dill or coriander. Fennel attracts many beneficial insects, including hoverflies and parasitic wasps.

Lavender—*Lavandula angustifolia*—Perennial (zones 5–8)

Lavender has no known pests, and its violet blue flowers will attract butterflies. Its protective aroma is also valuable around brassicas. Its strong scent will mask the scent of cabbage and cauliflower and confuse pests like aphids. Lavender germinates slowly from seed, so it's much easier to add it to your garden by propagating it from cuttings. If you've planted it outdoors in a colder climate (below zone 5), cover it with mulch over the winter to provide it with some protection. Its smell is lovely, and the leaves can be gathered for sachets to repel moths. Lavender prefers a pH of 7 and well-drained soil. If both conditions are met, it can reach a height of 3 feet, and it will form a bushy shape.

Lemon Balm—*Melissa officinalis*—Perennial (zones 4–9)

Lemon balm probably possesses the sweetest fragrance of all the herbs. Its Latin name of *Melissa* is actually derived from the fact that lemon balm flowers attract bees with their nectar. (*Melissa* means "honey bee" in Greek.) The scent of lemon balm can also disguise edibles nearby. As lemon balm is related to mint, it's better to plant it in a container. Move the container among the edibles to utilize its protective qualities. If you'd prefer to plant it in the garden, just don't let the seeds germinate. Spread

Parsley

mulch around the plant each year, and it will stop new shoots from germinating.

Lovage—*Levisticum officinale*—Perennial (zones 4–8)

The leafy lovage plant grows to a height of 6 feet each summer, so it's best reserved for the center of a perennial garden. It blooms in summer with yellow flower clusters and attracts beneficial wasps, along with tomato hornworms. Divide it each season and either plant the divisions in a new spot, or pot it up for a gift. The whole plant can be used in the kitchen. With a taste similar to celery, the leaves can be added to salad, the stems in soup, and the seeds in bread.

Oregano—*Origanum vulgare*—Perennial (zones 5–9)

Oregano is best known for its aromatic repellant properties and for its ability to attract beneficial insects. It is best suited for a perennial flowerbed or in a movable pot near the brassicas, particularly cabbage. It can become invasive, so it should not be planted among edibles. Cut back the plant several times throughout the growing season, and dry the leaves. A popular herb in the kitchen, make sure to keep a jar of the crumbled leaves around for pizza topping.

Parsley—*Petroselinum crispum*—Biennial (zones 4–9)

Plant a patch of parsley near the asparagus, as parsley is believed to repel asparagus beetles. Leave the parsley in the garden in the fall, and it should overwinter and then bloom in the spring. The spring blossoms will attract parasitic wasps. If you're lucky, new parsley will grow from the fallen seeds. Depending on the variety, parsley will reach approximately a foot and a half in height.

Rosemary—*Rosmarinus officinalis*—Annual (Perennial in zones 7 and higher)

Rosemary's fragrance is reported to repel cabbage and carrot flies. In turn,

Rosemary and thyme

Purple sage in the foreground with rhubarb in the background

its flowers will attract pollinators. Rosemary only generally flowers in warmer climates, and as a perennial, it will grow into a standalone bush. Above zone 7, rosemary is better utilized as a companion plant in the edible garden.

Sage—*Salvia officinalis*—Perennial (zones 5–9)

Sage should be placed in the carrot and tomato bed, at the edge of a strawberry patch, or near cabbage. It is reputed among companion gardeners to repel cabbageworms, mask the scent of the cabbage plant, and deter carrot flies. It also reportedly strengthens the growth of tomato plants. Sage will also attract honeybees. Plant sage in a space that has full sun, and divide it every few years. The Latin name *salvia officinalis* indicates the culinary variety of sage, so be sure to check plant tags if you purchase. There are many other varieties that can be utilized in the perennial bed. Sage leaves possess a copious amount of medical uses, and it pairs well with fall dishes in the kitchen. Some even use small bags in their closets to keep away moths.

Southernwood—*Artemisia abrotanum*—Perennial (zones 5–8)

Southernwood provides a dual purpose for the gardener—it attracts bees and butterflies, and it will mask the scent of cabbage. It's also said to repel aphids from beans. Southernwood will reach a height of 4 feet, and it usually spreads

Chive flowers

about 18 inches wide. With branches similar to an evergreen, southernwood is often utilized in wreaths.

Spearmint—*Mentha spicata*—Perennial (zones 4–11)

The first thing you need to know about mint is that you should never, ever plant it directly in the garden, because it will never, ever leave. If you plant it in an enclosed container, always place a saucer underneath to prevent the roots from growing into the soil. Once secured in a definitive location, mint actually makes a delightful addition to a companion planted garden. There are a ridiculous amount of mint varieties—chocolate, peppermint, apple, and lime, among many others. Spearmint is the best choice for the garden if you can only have one. It will confuse aphids and protect nearby plants. Mint roots easily from cuttings, so try collecting additional varieties from fellow gardeners.

Summer Savory—*Satureja hortensis*—Annual—self-sows readily

Summer savory grows quite easily from seed, and you will probably only need to sow it once. Savory is often planted with beans and onions. Gardeners have noted that the taste of both seems sweeter when they are planted near savory. Savory also encourages onions to grow more vigorously, it may protect beans from Mexican bean beetles, and its flowers attract pollinators. Savory plants will reach a height of 18 inches, and 3 feet in diameter. After it blooms

with tiny pink flowers in midsummer, the leaves will curl and dry on the plant. Savory is also often paired with beans in the kitchen, and it's often described as a perfect culinary herb.

Winter Savory—*Satureja Montana*—Perennial (zones 5–11)

Although winter savory is not as well known as summer savory, it is similar in taste, but it has a stronger flavor. Its pungent scent will dissuade garden pests, and its flowers will attract pollinators. Winter savory is a particularly hardy perennial and will often thrive through a good portion of the winter season. Propagate this herb through cuttings, and cut back growth several times each season. Although winter savory is not invasive, it might be simpler to plant the herb in a movable container. Each season, it should act as a companion to brassicas, especially the ever susceptible cabbage. Only new growth should be harvested for culinary use. Older more woody stems are better suited for the compost heap.

French Tarragon—*Artemisia dracunculus*—Perennial (zones 5–8)

Tarragon's aroma is reputed to invigorate growth of companion planted vegetables. It has no known pests, and its scent also offers protective qualities. The plant will eventually reach a height of a foot and a half, and it will form a small bushy shape.

Russian tarragon often masquerades as French tarragon, and many plant nurseries sell the wrong form. French tarragon plants are aromatic and provide a pleasant taste for use in the kitchen. Russian tarragon has no taste and is often grown from seeds. French tarragon cannot be grown from seeds, as the plants rarely flower. Instead, this form of tarragon is propagated from cuttings. Although their appearance is quite similar, try smelling any tarragon plants before purchasing. The French tarragon will have a strong odor, and the leaves will taste like licorice.

Thyme—*Thyme vulgaris*—Perennial (zones 5–9)

Thyme is honestly one of my favorite herbs in the garden. Its flavor is delicious in the kitchen, its flowers attract honeybees by dozens, and its low growing habit makes it ideal for edging. Studies have shown that it is also effective at masking the smell of nearby edibles and confusing those pests that seek out plants by smell.

Thyme prefers full sun and well-drained soil. Thyme plants will only reach 5-8 inches tall so plant them in a location where they won't by shaded by taller plants. Thyme will produce prolific white or purple flowers. Although thyme is perennial, in colder climates, it will benefit from some winter mulch protection. Divide the plants every few years. If the branches grow woody and tough, it is time for them to be divided.

Thyme comes in many wonderful varieties, including lemon, orange, coconut, lime, or nutmeg. Don't limit your garden to just one kind.

Sweet Marjoram—*Origanum majorana*—Annual in northern gardens—Perennial (zones 9–11)

Growing sweet marjoram near companion vegetables may improve their flavor, so it makes an easy and obvious addition to the companion planted garden. Sweet marjoram will reach a height of 3 feet, and it produces tiny closely knotted flowers in midsummer. It's often called "sweet" because it tastes like a milder version of oregano or thyme.

Let your dill plant flower towards the end of the season for beneficial insects.

Eastern carpenter bee

Chapter 8

INSECTS IN THE GARDEN

Black swallowtail caterpillar

Small black leaf beetle

Brown stink bug

Grasshopper

As I transitioned my style of gardening towards companion planting, I witnessed an explosion in the population of insect life in my garden. Damsel flies whirred by my shoulders, ladybugs greeted me perched on the edges of plant leaves, beetles scurried away every time I moved a bit of soil, and the bees, well, the bees were everywhere! I really began to take note of how many insects were in my garden, and how many kinds of insects I had invited to stay. I also sought to identify the garden insects I had attracted and comprehend exactly how they contributed to my garden's success. The following categories examine the role these insects might play in your garden, where you might see them, and any specific identifying characteristics.

Predatory insects are tiny hunters; they are a regiment of insects at your side to help you combat pests. Armed with pincers, piercers, and poisons, they are very capable, and as hunting is a natural instinct, they need little encouragement.

The manner in which predatory insects take down their victims rivals the storyline of any horror movie. Some predatory insects crush their prey

Soldier beetle

with mandibles. Others pierce them with their jaws or beaks, paralyze them with venom and suck out the "body juice." Tiger beetles will lie in wait in tiny holes, and wait patiently, even days or weeks, for prey to stroll by. When an unsuspecting insect comes too close, they snap forward at blinding speed, and attack.

Praying Mantis carve out their own territory for their hunting escapades. It's likely that you'll only see one in your garden, and it may even turn its head to give you a once over. While praying mantis are often friendly to humans, they will take down Japanese beetles, and many other pests, by grasping them with their powerful legs, and then eating the beetles alive. Ladybugs or beetles will breed more rapidly when they've noticed a high density of aphids.

The aggressive hunting instinct of predatory insects explains why they're bestowed with names like pirate, soldier, or assassin. The following three charts describe most of the more common garden predators.

Ladybugs on tomatillos

Predatory Insects				
Beetles—The number of beetle species in the world is unknown, but estimates range between 400,000 and 1 million. Beetles represent 40 percent of all insects. Most beetles have two clearly defined wings that rest on their backs, a distinct head, and all have six legs.	**Name**	**Description**	**Habitat**	**How they help**
	Fireflies *Lampyridae*	1/2 of an inch in length; brown or black in color; blinking "light" on abdomen that blinks when mating	Beneath decaying bark; will blink light at night; often found near woods	Eat insects, slugs, snails; hunt at night
	Ground Beetles *Carabidae*	3/4 to 1 inch long; black or brown in color; shiny; distinct legs	Under rocks, logs, boards, ground covers, and in brush; they will bite if disturbed	Eat many insects, aphids, cabbage worms, Colorado potato beetles, cutworms, diamondback moths, flea beetles, root maggots, and many others
	Ladybugs/Lady Beetles *Coccinellidae*	1/16 to 3/8 of an inch long; colored red, yellow, tan, or orange; black spots; oval in shape	On flowers like alfalfa, dandelions, goldenrod, daisies, zinnias; edibles like brassicas and artichokes	Larvae eat aphids, thrips, mites, and mealy bugs, adults eat aphids also
	Rove Beetles *Staphylinidae*	1/10 to 1 inch long; black and brown, antenna in front; pinchers to grasp victims	In the compost pile, under leaf mulch, or wooden boards; in clover, will pinch if disturbed	Eat all kinds of maggots
	Soldier/Leatherwing Beetles *Cantharidae*	1/3 to 1/2 of an inch long; long brown, orange, or tan bodies, black spots behind head and on wings	On daisies, cosmos, sunflowers, and wildflowers like goldenrod or milkweed	Larvae are predators to grasshopper eggs, adults eat aphids and other soft-bodied insects
	Tiger Beetles *Cicindelidae/ Carabinae*	1/2 to 3/4 of an inch long; bronze, green, gray, and black; fast movers; grab prey with clawlike mandibles that hook onto prey; around 100 species	Love sandy surfaces; some are nocturnal; burrow into the ground; under perennials and ground cover	Adults eat ants, flies, caterpillars, and aphids

Predatory Insects				
	Name	**Description**	**Habitat**	**How they help**
Bugs—Bugs are more varied in their size and shape. Most have triangularly shaped backs and suck fluid from their prey.	Ambush Bugs *Phymatidae*	1/2 an inch long; light yellow, green and brown; 300 species	Yellow and white wildflowers; like asters and goldenrod	Wait for prey to wander by and pounce; eat flies, butterflies
	Assassin Bugs *Reduviidae*	1/2 to 3/4 of an inch long; oval shaped bugs; use beak to pierce prey; can bite	Goldenrod, trees, shrubs, and hedgerow, under ground cover	Feed on aphids, flying insects, asparagus beetle eggs
	Big-Eyed Bugs *Lygaeidae*	1/8 to 1/4 of an inch long; gray and brown; large eyes; oval shaped; often possess distinctive black markings	Most are found in the south and on the west coast; found among ground cover; overwinter in garden debris	Eat aphids, blister beetles, eggs, and leafhoppers
	Damsel Bugs *Nabidae*	3/8 to 1/2 of an inch long; gray or brown; long antenna and legs; flat	Found in ground cover; more likely found in fields than a home garden	Eat aphids, caterpillars, thrips, leafhoppers, among many others
	Minute Pirate Bugs *Orius spp.*	Itsy bitsy—1/4 of an inch; black tipped wings; oval shaped; needle shaped beaks	Live in ground cover and sometimes on daisies; throughout N. America	Eat all kinds of pests; aphids, thrips, leafhoppers, and corn earworm eggs; also eat pollen
	Spined Soldier Bugs *Podisus maculiventris*	1/2 of an inch long; flat and angular; gray or brown; similar to a stink bug, but with pointy shoulders	In the perennial garden; throughout N. America	Eat Mexican bean beetles, Colorado potato beetles, and the larvae of many pests
	Two Spotted Stink Bug *Perillus bioculatus*	3/8 to 1/2 of an inch long; bright contrasting black and orangey markings	In asparagus patch, or among weeds	Eat eggs and larvae of many pests
Dragonflies—There are about 450 kinds of dragonflies in North America; most are distinguished by their slender bodies and wide wingspan.	Darners *Aeschnidae*	2 1/2 to 3 inches long with a wing span of up to 5 inches; blue and black spotted bodies	On water surfaces; near streams; throughout N. America	Eat mosquitoes and mosquito larvae
	Narrow-Winged Damselflies *Coenagrionidae*	1 to 2 inches long; screen-like wings; shiny blue with bug eyes	Water surfaces; ponds, streams	Eat mosquitoes and aphids

Predatory Insects				
Lacewings—These insects are characterized by their delicate transparent wings.	**Name**	**Description**	**Habitat**	**How they help**
	Brown Lacewings *Hemerobiidae*	1/4 to 3/8 of an inch long; brown with transparent wings; tiny heads	Nocturnal; woods or fields	Eat aphids
	Green Lacewings *Chrysopiade*	1/2 of an inch long; pale green; transparent wings, small heads	They eat nectar, so you may find them among perennials like Queen Anne's Lace, or yarrow; or in meadows	Eat hundreds of aphids and many pests, including thrips, leafhoppers, and Colorado potato beetles; sometimes, they do eat each other
Flies—Although a few flies are known to humans because they bite, most actually benefit the garden through predatory activity or pollination.	Aphid Midges/ Gallflies *Cecidomyiidae*	1/16 of an inch long; look like mosquitoes, but much smaller; orange larvae	On flowers that aphids eat, adults are nocturnal; need to have flowers around to stay	Eat aphids
	Robber Flies *Asilidae*	1/2 to 3/4 of an inch long; variety within species; often gray; large black eyes; bristly beards; distinct separate wings	Among decayed wood and leaf mold	Will ambush pests and beneficials; larvae eat maggots and grubs
Mantids	Praying Mantis *Mantis religiosa*	2 inches in length; triangular shaped head that can turn, long front legs that can be held in a "praying" position; green or tan	Usually only see one in garden; jump all around the garden; found more often in the eastern N. America	Eat both pests and beneficials
Mites	Predatory Mites *Phytoseiidae*	Microscopic in size; red bodies	Hide around the garden; hard to see with the naked eye	Attack all kinds of pests, thrips, and spider mites
Spiders—There are 3,000 species of spiders in North America, and very, very few are after you! Spiders (arachnids) are in your garden to trap insects.	Crab Spiders *Thomisidae*	1/2 inch long; rounded backsides and large clawlike legs; often match the flowers they hide in; I've seen pink and white spiders in cosmos	Hide among flowers; favor yellow and white blossoms found throughout N. America	Attack all kinds of insects
	Orb Weavers *Araneidae*	1/2 to 1 inch long; brown with black stripes on legs; eight eyes; many species	Generate webs around the garden	Catch jumping insects in webs
	Wolf Spiders *Lycosidae*	1/8 to 1 1/8 inch long; brown or gray; two light stripes down body; 200 species	Hide under mulch; will carry white sacs of eggs with them; nocturnal	Eat pests and beneficials, aphids, mites, moths and beetles

Pollinators make it possible for your fruiting vegetables to reach optional productivity. Most of the foods you cultivate in your garden require pollination. Pollinators seek out garden flowers to eat nectar. They also are there to attract mates and will utilize the "floral oils" generated by flowering plants. These insects pollinate accidentally. As they visit flowers, pollen rubs on their bodies—they will then carry that pollen from plant to plant.

To attract pollinators to your garden, pick perennial flowers that showcase large clusters of blooms and an extended blooming time. Pollinators are the easiest to spot in the garden because many are most active during the daytime and during warm weather. (Most moths are nocturnal.)

We noticed an increase in pollination once we started keeping honeybees. Here, Tim's inspecting the hive.

Pollinators				
Bees—There are 20,000 species of bees. You will find both native and exotic bees in your garden, and you should plant flowers that attract native bees and the European honey bee.	**Name**	**Description**	**Habitat**	**How they help**
	Bumblebees *Bombus spp.*	1/2 to 3/4 of an inch; Fuzzy bees with black and yellow bodies	Build colonies in abandoned nests of birds; often seen buzzing around flowers	Pollinate garden crops, flowers, and blueberry bushes
	Honeybees *Apis mellifera*	Worker bees measure 3/8 to 3/4 of an inch; black stripes, brown and yellow; were introduced to N. America during Columbian Exchange	Can be encouraged by keeping bee hives; also naturalized in the wild; found in tree trunks	Pollinate many garden crops, flowers, and fruiting trees
	Solitary bees *Andrena spp. and Panurginus spp.*	400 species in North America; include mason bees and leafcutter bees	Build nests in small holes in rotting trees, will also build nests in wood drilled with holes	Pollinate flowering plants, love asters
	Ground-Nesting Bees	Include digger bees, sweat bees, and mining bees	Solo bees that dig ant-like holes in the ground	
Butterflies—Very popular insects because of their beauty, are most often seen during the summer months of warm weather	Brushfooted Nymphalidae family	210 species in N. America; large, upper wings display bright colors; great diversity in size and color; include monarchs and painted ladies	Many plants, sunflowers, hollyhocks, lupine, Jerusalem artichokes. Monarch feed only on milkweed	Larvae can chew leaves of food plants, but only minimally; adults are pollinators
	Skippers Hesperiidae family	300 species in N. America; orangey brown, small size, antennas have thicker bent bulbed end	Meadows and the edges of the woods, many like members of the legume family	
	Swallowtail Papilionidae family	40 species in N. America; several kinds, some black with yellow dots, some striped yellow and black, others cream, black, with blue tips	Fields, meadows, many prefer plants of the apiaceae family, especially where flowers are abundant	
Flies	Hoverflies/Flowerflies *Syrphidae*	1/2 to 5/8 of an inch long; black and yellow striped	Quickly flit around flowers; eat honeydew; need flowers to stay	Adults are pollinators—need blossoms to attract; larvae eat aphids, leafhoppers, corn ear-worms, and many more pests
	Bee flies Bombyliidae family	300 species, thick and hairy, stripes colored black, white, or brown, spotted wings	Woodlands and the edges of wooded areas	Larvae are parasitoids of other insects; adults are pollinators

Eastern
carpenter bee
visiting some
hairy mountain
mint

A honeybee on anise hyssop

Black swallowtail caterpillar

Skipper

Black swallowtail butterfly

Black swallowtail caterpillar on parsley

Parasitoid insects spend a portion of their lives growing on or inside the body of a host. These insects will attach to the host when they lay eggs on host eggs, larva, or they might even insert their eggs into full-grown insects. Once the parasitoid eggs hatch, the larva will then feed on the hosts as they grow. Aphidiid wasps will eat the interior of their aphid hosts, and then emerge once they've reached adulthood. The easiest way to spot the work of the aphidiid wasp is to look for a pile of dead aphids. Some species of beneficial beetles also exhibit parasitoid characteristics.

These insects most commonly attack pests, and they rarely go after beneficial insects. Most have a specific pest that suits their fancy.

Parasitoids				
Flies	**Name**	**Description**	**Habitat**	**How they help**
	Tachinid Flies *Tachinidae*	1/3 to 1/2 of an inch long; similar to houseflies; gray or tan	Find their cocoons on caterpillars; also found on wildflowers; throughout N. America	Parasitoids of corn borers, cabbage worms, squash bugs, potato beetles, and many others, (including their own mothers on occasion); also pollinate
Wasps	Aphidiid Wasps *Aphidiinae*	1/8 of an inch long; black; like elongated houseflies	Found throughout the U.S; hard to spot in garden	Larvae eat the interior of aphids, pupate, and then emerge out of the bodies as adults
	Braconid Wasps *Braconidae*	3/8 of an inch long; thin bodies; black upper bodies and red lower bodies	Most likely to see them in their cocoon on caterpillars	Attach onto all kinds of pests; including hornworms, corn borers, and armyworms
	Chalcid Wasps *Chalcididae*	1/16 to 3/8 of an inch long; shiny blue or green	Found all over the garden and in perennials	Lay eggs inside of caterpillars; feed on whiteflies, aphids, leafhoppers and caterpillars
	Ichneumonid Wasps *Ichneumonidae*	From 1/4 of an inch up to 1 5/8 of an inch long; thousands of species, large "tail" that inserts eggs into prey	Around the bug baths, nocturnal, cocoon inside caterpillars	The adults insert eggs into caterpillars and the adult will grow from within

Common garden insect pests

In my plant-by-plant guide, I describe the most common pests that attack specific plant species. However, there are some garden pests that are more indiscriminate when choosing their victims. Many organic gardeners reduce pest populations by hand picking pests, squashing eggs, or implementing floating row covers.

If one were to read a sampling of gardening literature these days, it would appear that gardeners spend most of their time in the garden battling insect pests. Whole garden books are devoted to techniques that have been devised to eradicate pest infestations. Honestly, most of these insects have made such little impact on my garden that I wouldn't have even noticed them unless I decided to look. Companion planting keeps nature in balance. I decided to include specific descriptions here because I think it's important to have an awareness of the biodiversity in your garden. Please don't see the following words as instructions to seek and destroy.

Aphids—*Aphididae*

Aphids are minutely sized insects measuring only 1/6 of an inch to 3/8 of an inch in length. While most are colored green or black, others can be pink, brown, gray, or blue. When aphids attack plants, they will suck the juice. The leaves will lose their vigor, curl and yellow, and eventually drop. As the plant weakens from the attack, it will lessen its fruit and flower production. The secretion excreted from the aphids is called honeydew. The honeydew is often eaten by ants, and it can cause black mold to grow on infected plants that will prevent photosynthesis.

Thankfully, aphids are a favorite among predatory insects, especially ladybugs. They can also be knocked from an infested plant with a quick blast from a forceful water hose. Aphids don't like odorous herbs like chives, mint, catnip, or alliums.

Likely Victims:

Aphids aren't picky eaters. They suck the sap from a wide range of vegetables and fruit plants, flowers, bushes, and trees.

Cutworms—*Noctuidae*

Cutworms are dastardly demons that can dash a new gardener's hopes and dreams in a single night. The worms are actually the larvae of a night flying moth. They inflict their damage by chewing through the stems of young seedlings or transplants.

Predatory insects will eat cutworms, but I've found that the best way to ensure protection for my young transplants is to surround them with a small barrier. I've used newspaper and toilet paper rolls, but my favorite barrier involved reusing old cat food tin cans with the bottoms removed. Newspaper must be cut and rolled around each plant, and it slows down planting day. I keep my tin cans from year to year, and plunk them down around each seedling once they are in the ground. Make sure to lightly push each can into the soil so that an inch remains above the ground.

Likely Victims:

Cutworms will attack any plant with a singular stem—like peppers, tomatoes, or broccoli.

Japanese beetle

Earwigs—*Forficula auricularia*

Earwigs can be classified as beneficial insects and as pests. They're a predator to aphids and nematodes, but they will also eat tiny holes in leaves, and sometimes, in fruit. They measure 1/2 of an inch to an inch in length, and they are brownish red with pinchers at the end of a curling tail.

Before setting a trap for the earwig, weigh the damage they've inflicted against their overall benefit in the garden. Most earwigs will only impose a trifling amount of disruption. Trap earwigs by placing a tubelike structure in proximity to their feeding area. A rolled up newspaper, piece of bamboo, or a cardboard tube will work fine. The insects feed at night, so pick up the tubes and empty them in the morning.

Likely Victims:

Earwigs munch on lettuce, strawberries, corn silk, and numerous flowers.

Leafhoppers— *Cicadelliade*

Leafhoppers are 1/4 of an inch in length and appear in a wide range of colors, including brown, yellow and green. They "hop" from plant to plant and attack plants by sucking plant juice from leaves. You can spot their damage by looking for white spots on the leaves. Plants with extensive damage will have wilted, yellowed leaves and stunted growth. They can survive the winter in piles of garden debris.

Ladybugs, lacewings, and pirate bugs all attack the eggs and larvae of leafhoppers.

Likely Victims:

Leafhoppers favor beans, beets, lettuce, and potatoes.

Japanese Beetles— *Papillia japonica*

Japanese beetles are probably the most visible garden pests. They measure 1/2 an inch in length as adults, and they have metallic green backs with bronze wings. The beetles eat foliage of all kinds and sometimes small fruit like raspberries. They are often found in mass numbers munching and mating on a tree, shrub, or garden edible. Most Japanese beetles live in the eastern portion of the United States.

If a plant is shaken, the beetles will protectively drop to the ground. To slow their progress, take a bucket of soapy water, and gradually knock the beetles into the bucket. Try to repeat this process every few days until the beetle population appears to have been reduced.

Likely Victims:

Japanese beetles will attack a wide range of leaves, flowers, and fruits.

Root Knot Nematodes/ Eelworms—*Nematoda*

Nematodes most often live in the soil. They are often microscopically sized, however some can reach up to 1/4 of an inch. Some help gardeners by feeding on pests or breaking down decomposing organic material in the compost pile. Others attack plant matter by injecting saliva, and then sucking out softened tissue. You won't really see the nematodes in action; instead, you will witness the results of their feasts. Crops damaged by nematodes will most likely turn yellow, and their growth will be anemic. The roots will be riddled with lesions or nodules, or showcase an excessive amount of root growth. Some also carry damaging viruses.

Nematodes are not the average garden pest. If you've seen signs of their damage, you might have to let the infected beds lay fallow for a year to starve them from the bed. Some studies have noted that nematode populations can be significantly reduced by planting marigolds as a cover crop, and then turning them under at the end of the growing season. To avoid this predicament, remember to always rotate your crops from year to year.

Likely Victims:

Parasitic nematodes will attack most plants, likely any plant with a root.

Slugs—*Mollusca*

Slugs slink around wet shady sections of the garden—under low growing vegetation or wooden boards. Although you might not spot the slugs, you will see the slime trails they leave as they slither, and giant holes in your leaves from their binge eating. Slugs are from the mollusk family and can range in size and length. Most measure around 1 inch long, although some reach 7 or 8 inches.

Gardeners have developed ingenious methods to deal with slug infestations. Slugs will be distracted away from your edibles by a shallow tin can full of beer. If you find your beer too valuable to feed to the slugs, try placing wooden boards around infected areas. The slugs will congregate under the boards at night, and can be picked off in the early morning. Slugs are also deterred with a copper border (it

will shock the slugs), or with a sprinkling of lime, crushed seashells or coffee grounds.

Slugs also possess many natural predators. Toads eat slugs, so add a toad home to your strawberry beds. Predatory insects like ground beetles and fireflies will also eat slugs. Slugs favor red clover more than most anything else, so try planting the cover crop as a trap crop.

Likely Victims:

Slugs eat beans, strawberries, and all kinds of salad greens.

Thrips/Thunder flies—*Thysanoptera*

Thrips are slender insects that generally measure less than 1/2 of an inch in length and have fringed wings. Some thrips will attack other pests, but others will attack plants and they can also carry disease.

Likely Victims:

Thrips aren't picky about their prey. They are noted for eating onions, beans, carrots, and squash.

Root Maggots—*Delia*

Root maggots are 1/5 of an inch in length, pale yellow, and almost transparent in color. They bore into root vegetables, and the roots of vegetables, and create a network of tunnels that will cause the plant to yellow and even die.

Most infestations are avoided by rotating crops from year to year. Gardeners also sprinkle dried hot peppers around root crops to discourage the maggots.

Likely Victims:

Root maggots are found in onions, cabbage, radishes, carrots, and turnips, and they are more likely in northern gardens.

Milkweed borer

Egg mass of the three-lined potato beetle

Nurseries and online catalogs often tout boxes of beneficials that you can purchase, and then release into your garden. I've never found this to be necessary. Spend the money on flowers, and the insects will follow. Otherwise, without the necessary habitat, the insects will leave, or they will die off within a generation.

Wheel bug, a member of the assassin bug family

Chapter 9

KEEPING A GARDEN JOURNAL

I know I should be the perfect example of a gardener and tell you that I write in my garden journal every day. That I keep track of temperature, blooming times, and pounds harvested, that every piece of data that can be written down is written down. I admire gardeners who have this kind of time and tenacity. I don't.

Most of my garden journaling is completed in the off-season, and the northern New York climate affords me some luxury of time.

In late winter, I plan for the coming season, devise a seed-starting schedule, and map out my garden beds. In early spring, when the snow melts and the garden reveals itself, I make a list of projects to be completed. In the fall, I assess the successes and failures of the growing season.

Late Winter:

In late winter, as I order my seeds, I plan out our garden for the coming year. I determine what crops I want to grow, how much I need, and how the crops will be companion planted. I base these decisions by reviewing the notes I'd taken in the previous fall.

I also create a month-by-month chart to outline what crops will be planted in each bed for every month. Some crops, like sweet potatoes, or Brussels sprouts, might dwell in the same bed for the entire growing season. Others, like spinach, carrots, or radishes, often make an appearance in one bed in the spring, and another during fall. By planning this aspect of my gardening, I'm not scrambling during the season to come up with a succession-planting schedule.

Month-by-month planning also helps me to keep track of our garden beds from year to year. To conform to crop rotation guidelines, I try to avoid planting the same family of edibles in a bed for four years. Although I might be able to remember the layout of the garden from the previous season, my brain struggles to remember any specific garden layout over successive seasons. With my month-by-month calendar, I can easily compare each year.

Finally, when I first started growing my own seeds, I developed a calendar to remind myself about seed starting, transplant, and direct sowing. It took me some time to generate this schedule the first year, but because it is not "date" dependent, it has lasted each successive year with only minor revisions.

To help you work through my technique, I've outlined plans for a small four-bed garden (below) based on the zone we live in—5A. For the example, I chose four beds I designed for my plant-by-plant guide. After you choose your beds, you might replace some plants based on your own preferences.

With the planting schedule, I draw up a chart for each month of my gardening year. I assign crops to each bed for each month of the growing season. You'll notice that I also included some "season extenders," along with the crops included in the graphic (italics). Any potential cover crop area is also listed (bold). I try to plant a cover crop between any heavy feeders, so buckwheat follows the spring brassicas, and a fall *Green Manure Mix* from Johnny's Selected Seeds is planted in the fall in two of the beds.

Obviously, this chart does necessitate some flexibility. My bush beans might produce longer than I had planned, or frost might arrive earlier than expected. Our garden has 30 beds at the moment, so planning out the season in advance is almost a requirement. I type my plan each year, so I can "cut and paste" my plans without having to start from scratch.

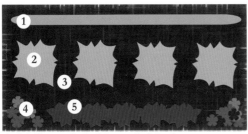

1 - Pole Beans 3 - Radishes 5 - Spinach
2 - Cucumbers 4 - Nasturtiums

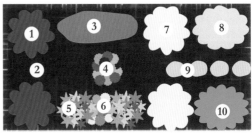

1 - Broccoli 5 - Zinnias 8 - Thyme
2 - Cabbage 6 - Calendulas 9 - Kohlrabi
3 - Dill 7 - Cauliflower 10 - Parsley
4 - Marigolds

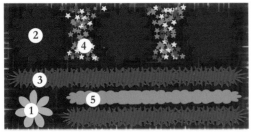

1 - Pepper 3 - Onions 5 - Carrots
2 - Tomato 4 - Borage

1 - Bush Beans 3 - Basil
2 - Marigolds 4 - Eggplant

4-Bed Companion Planting Layout

Month-by-Month Planting Schedule

	April	May	June	July	Aug.	Sept.	Oct.	Nov.
1 4 x 8	*Spinach* *Mache* *Tatsoi*	Spinach Pole Beans Radishes	Cucumbers Radishes Spinach Nasturtiums	Cucumbers Pole Beans Nasturtiums	Cucumbers Pole Beans Nasturtiums	Cucumbers Pole Beans Nasturtiums	**Fall "Green Manure" Mix**	**Fall "Green Manure" Mix**
2 4 x 8	**Winter Rye** (till in 3 weeks before planting)	Broccoli Cabbage Cauliflower Kohlrabi Dill Marigolds Zinnias Calendulas Thyme (Per.) Parsley (Per.)	Broccoli Cabbage Cauliflower Kohlrabi Dill Marigolds Zinnias Calendulas Thyme Parsley	Cabbage Cauliflower Dill Marigolds Zinnias Calendulas Thyme Parsley	**Buckwheat** Dill Marigolds Zinnias Calendulas Thyme Parsley	**Buckwheat** Dill Marigolds Zinnias Calendulas Thyme Parsley	**Buckwheat** Dill Marigolds Zinnias Calendulas Thyme Parsley	*Spinach* *Mache* *Tatsoi* Thyme Parsley
3 4 x 8	Carrots Onions	Carrots Onions Peppers Tomatoes Borage	Carrots Onions Peppers Tomatoes Borage	Carrots Onions Peppers Tomatoes Borage	Onions Peppers Tomatoes Borage	Peppers Tomatoes Borage	Peppers Tomatoes Borage	
4 4 x 8		Bush Beans Basil Marigolds	Bush Beans Eggplant Basil Marigolds	Bush Beans Eggplant Basil Marigolds	Lettuce Eggplant Basil Marigolds	Lettuce Eggplant Basil Marigolds	**Fall "Green Manure" Mix**	**Fall "Green Manure" Mix**

Seed Starting Schedule

Most of the seeds that I start indoors are planted on the weekends. Seeds are started from February to May, and I also seed a couple of fall crops at the end of June. Instead of creating a new plan for seed starting each year, I made a weekly seed-starting chart that wasn't date specific, and could be carried over each gardening season. The seed starting chart on page 129 would work with my four-bed example.

Early Spring:

In early spring, when I can actually see the garden and walk around it without snowshoes, I make a list of projects I'd like to complete within the year.

The list is always idealistic, and honestly, I don't think I've had a year where I could cross everything off. Most often, if I am able to draw a line through a task, I then spend the next minute writing a new task at the bottom of the list.

I've created an example list for you below to get you started.

Potential projects to be completed:

- Move, divide, re-pot perennials as needed
- List new perennials to be planted during the season—determine source
- Build small pond for toads, frogs, and birds
- Build any trellises, garden gates, or fences
- Prune trees and shrubs as necessary—remove any damaged wood
- Assess compost situation—build new piles as necessary, always be on the lookout for possible materials
- Any additional beds to be built or modified
- Plan for season extenders, make garden hoops, build a cold frame

Late Fall:

When my gardening season reaches a close, I ask myself the following questions.

- Were there any crops where you grew too much? Too little?
- Was the amount of space provided appropriate for each plant?
- Which varieties grew the best? Were there any that failed? (Germination rate was poor, plants grew too slowly for the climate, variety taste was bland, etc.)
- Were there any crops that you *just didn't like*?
- If you did design your own companion planting combinations, make sure to take note of their relative success.

As you work through this list, make sure to write down your observations. Try to go through the questions more than once and consult with anyone who helped you during the growing season. I've found that I need to work through this list at least twice before I've answered everything satisfactorily.

Gardening offers the opportunity to start fresh every year. Once the patterns established here become ingrained in your gardening routine, create your own experiments. Even if they're a miserable failure, you'll document the flaws once the season ends, and adjust your approach for the following season.

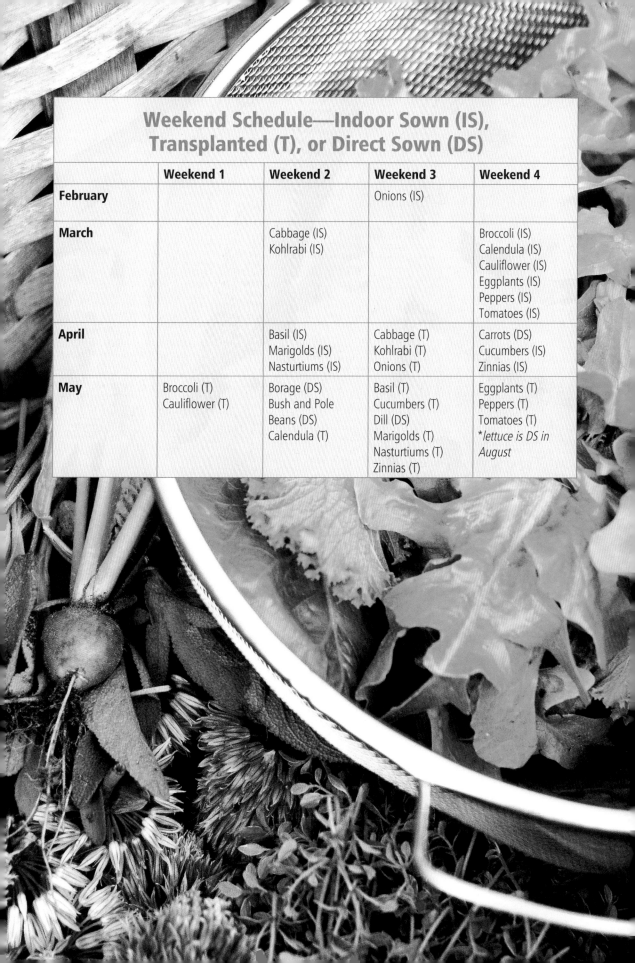

Weekend Schedule—Indoor Sown (IS), Transplanted (T), or Direct Sown (DS)

	Weekend 1	Weekend 2	Weekend 3	Weekend 4
February			Onions (IS)	
March		Cabbage (IS) Kohlrabi (IS)		Broccoli (IS) Calendula (IS) Cauliflower (IS) Eggplants (IS) Peppers (IS) Tomatoes (IS)
April		Basil (IS) Marigolds (IS) Nasturtiums (IS)	Cabbage (T) Kohlrabi (T) Onions (T)	Carrots (DS) Cucumbers (IS) Zinnias (IS)
May	Broccoli (T) Cauliflower (T)	Borage (DS) Bush and Pole Beans (DS) Calendula (T)	Basil (T) Cucumbers (T) Dill (DS) Marigolds (T) Nasturtiums (T) Zinnias (T)	Eggplants (T) Peppers (T) Tomatoes (T) *lettuce is DS in August*

Chapter 10

A PLANT-BY-PLANT GUIDE TO COMPANION PLANTING

For each plant in the following section, I've divided the guide into six main sections—friends, for companion planting, to grow, to harvest, foes, and seed possibilities. I've tried my best to parse the essential growing requirements for each plant. I want you to have confidence in your garden and not give up before you even start.

In the "companion planting possibilities" section, I've drawn some companion planted beds to help you organize your garden. I remember taking my gardening books out with me to the garden during my first years as a gardener and just sitting on the ground trying to figure out what to plant where. I spent entirely too much time confused by the directions and found myself spending more time reading than planting. The beds I've suggested are intended to get you to your planting and seeding straightaway without having to spend hours flipping through the pages of this book.

The beds I've drawn out are just suggestions. Each bed is laid out in a 4' by 8' space unless otherwise noted. I chose this size because many beds are built with these parameters. These plans can be extended, shortened, or redrawn to fit more creatively shaped beds. As you develop your gardening skills, you can construct your own bed designs. I included the list of "plant friends" with each crop for this purpose. As a general rule, keep in mind that plants are much more likely to be friends than foes. Unless I've specifically mentioned a poor pairing, the plants will probably get along just fine.

In the "to grow" and "to harvest" sections I focus on seeding, planting, spacing, fertilizing, and any other necessary information to start your plants and to keep them healthy and strong. Although harvesting might seem blatantly obvious, I give some tips regarding overlooked edibles, and when crops are most likely at their peak.

In the "foe" section, I consciously made an effort to focus on the essentials. I've tried my best not to overwhelm this section with unnecessary details. I don't feel that gardening books should list every possible setback. For new gardeners, an overtly detailed book can make the act of gardening appear to be fraught with danger.

I promise, although there are many possible hazards described, you probably will never notice most of the pests I've recorded, and it's very unlikely that your plants will be attacked by every disease in existence.

I also included a "seed possibility" guide to help you narrow down your choices from among the abundance of options presented in seed catalogs. Although I gave some special consideration to our own personal favorites, I also tried to choose varieties that produce well in many areas of the country, and varieties that work well for small gardens.

Beans—*Phaseolus vulgaris*

Ideal P.H.—6.0-6.5
Feed—soil builder
Light requirements—full
Family—legume

Friends:

Vegetables and Fruits: beets, cabbage, carrots, cauliflower, celery, corn, cucumbers, eggplants, radishes, potatoes, and tomatoes*

Herbs and Flowers: borage, catnip, chamomile, dill, sage, savory, marigolds and nasturtiums

* pole beans work best with corn, potatoes, and radishes, and members of the cucurbit family

To Grow:

Bean seeds germinate after the ground temperature has reached at least 60 degrees. Wait until after the danger of frost has passed before planting them outdoors. Bush beans can be planted throughout the summer. Read the back of your seed packets carefully before planning which seeds to plant when. The range of days from planting to maturity can vary wildly among bean varieties. If you're planting later in the season for a fall crop, add a week on to the "days until maturity."

I tend to add a few bush bean seeds wherever I have room, and many bean seeds have made their way into my front flowerbeds. Pole beans only need to be planted once, though those in warmer climates can plant a second succession.

Each seed should be planted about 2-3 inches apart in the ground, at a depth between 1 and 2 inches. As the seedlings

All legumes add nitrogen to the soil, and their roots can act as a green manure.

To make use of the roots within your garden soil, don't pull the plants from the ground at the end of the season. Instead, just cut them at the root level, and gently till the roots back into the ground.

emerge, they should be thinned so that they are 3 to 4 inches apart.

Pole beans will need some sort of trellis for support. Be creative when deciding on

For Companion Planting

1. To maximize yield in a companion planted bed, try seeding pole beans along the back side of a bed. In front of the pole beans, seed some cucumber hills. Around the cucumber add spinach and radishes. Once the spring vegetables are pulled, plant some carrots in the open space for a late fall harvest. Plant some nasturtiums or marigolds along the edges. (With this example, the pole beans and the cucumbers would need trellising.)

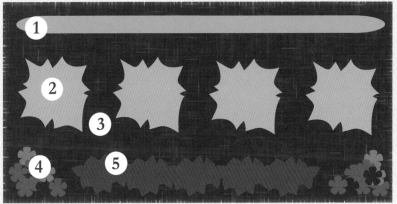

1 - Pole Beans   3 - Radishes   5 - Spinach
2 - Cucumbers   4 - Nasturtiums

2. Beans also grow well with tomatoes, the beans provide nitrogen for the tomatoes, and according to a scientific study, the yield per plant will increase when the two are paired. Add some borage or marigolds to fill the spaces in between, or some spinach along the edges.

1 - Bush Beans 3 - Tomatoes
2 - Marigolds   4 - Peppers

3. Other options: A scientific study indicated that pole beans were less damaged by disease when they were interplanted with corn. To see how pole beans might work with the "three sisters method" of companion planting, including corn and beans, turn to page 158. For an example, bed grid with interplanted bush beans, marigolds, celery and potatoes, turn to page 198.

a trellis. Simple trellises can be made from wire, metal poles, thin boards, twine, or long sticks. I've also seen ladders repurposed as trellises, and pole beans climbing along the front railing of a porch.

Weeds are not generally numerous around bean plants because the leaves of the plants shade the soil. However, bean plants do require consistent and even moisture once they've formed flowers. A side dressing of mulch after the plants have reached about a foot tall can offer better moisture consistency.

> When your bean plants are flush with flowers, pinch the tops off the plant. The beans will then propel their energy towards bean production.

To Harvest:

For fresh beans, pick them when they're tender on the vine, and right as the bean seeds have started to show through the pod. If beans are picked in a timely manner, every other day or so, the plants will continue to produce for several weeks.

If you've decided to grow a crop of dried beans, the pods should be left to dry on the vine. They will turn brown and take on a brittle texture, and the beans will separate from the pod. Shell the dried beans (or give them to your kids to shell), and place them in an open mason jar covered with cheesecloth until they are thoroughly dry. When dry, they will make a satisfying rattling sound if shaken. Close the jar with a canning lid and keep the beans on a pantry shelf.

> Beans and other legumes are often described as a "nitrogen fixing" crop. This means that legume roots actually collect nitrogen from the soil. Rhizobacteria settle on the roots of the beans and draw in nitrogen from the soil. The nitrogen they collect will transform into a type of nitrogen that can be utilized by the plants. This process is often referred to as nitrogen "fixing."

Foes:

The Mexican Bean Beetle—Mexican bean beetles are tiny little beetles that measure only 1/4 of an inch. They have tan backs with little dots, and they are sometimes mistaken for lady beetles.

Mexican bean beetles will eat holes in the leaves of bean plants, and they can reduce the plants' production if allowed to multiply. If you spot leaves that look like a framework of veins, the Mexican bean beetle has likely stopped by to snack. The larvae can be "hand squished" on the undersides of the leaves to discourage further destruction. Their damage is reduced spectacularly when beans are interplanted with other vegetables and herbs, so make sure to use your companion plant skills when adding beans to your garden.

Bean rust can also attack plants when the plants have been spaced too close together, when they haven't received sufficient sunlight, or when the climate has been wetter than usual. The rust will create dark brown freckles on the leaves. To eradicate the rust, make sure

> The types of beans typically grown in American gardens originate from the Americas. Sometimes, these beans are referred to as French beans, thus confusing their origins even further. Beyond French beans, there is a multitude of diversity within the bean species, and they vary among taste, texture, and growing requirements. If you've mastered the growing requirements for French beans, try edamame beans, runner beans (*Scarlet Emperors* have gorgeous flowers that attract hummingbirds), or the curious quarter-sized *Christmas Lima* beans.

to thin the inflicted crops and rotate for the future.

Beans, like other legumes, do not like being planted with any type of allium. Pole beans dislike beets, kohlrabi, and sunflowers.

Although not required, beans and pea seeds yield more when they've been inoculated. When you inoculate, you're just sprinkling rhizobacteria on the seeds before they're planted. Although rhizobacteria are already present in the soil, inoculating the seeds will energize the seeds to maximize their growth. Inoculating will also improve the condition of the soil. More substantial root growth from inoculated seeds leads to better soil aeration and a great quantity of nutrients. Inoculants can be purchased at garden centers and online. If you decide to purchase some, consider dividing your purchase with friends. Most often inoculants are only sold in bulk, and they lose their vitality after a year.

SEED POSSIBILITIES:

I've never had luck freezing beans for winter, so most of the beans I grow are for fresh eating. I also let them dry on the vine and collect the seeds for chili, soups, or for slow simmering on the stove in winter.

For fresh eating:

Jade (OP)—tender, stringless beans; plants reach 18-22" in height; heat tolerant and not stressed by extreme temperatures; beans measure 5-7", and the plants will produce late into the season; bush habit—*55 days*

Kentucky Wonder (H)—incredibly productive heirloom variety; nutty flavor; should be picked when smaller; stringless pods measure 7-9" long; pole habit—*65-70 days*

Provider (OP)—very reliable variety that grows well in many climates; plants reach 2' in height and grow straight beans 5-8" in levngth; also demonstrates resistance to disease, bush habit—*50-55 days*

Rattlesnake (H)—dark green pods with streaks of purple; vines can reach up to 10' in height; versatile; can be eaten fresh but can also be left on the vine to dry; pole habit—*60-90 days*

Romano (OP)—exquisite dark purple pods with lovely lilac flowers; easy to grow; 5" pods; great taste; bush habit—*60 days*

For drying on the vine:

Cannellini (H)—prized Italian beans; smooth; rich flavor; mild taste; bush habit—*80 days (fresh)/100 days (dry)*

Good Mother Stallard (H)—maroon beans with white speckles; creamy and nutty texture; 5-6 beans per pod; pole habit—*85-95 days (dry)*

Lazy Housewife (H)—straight, stringless pods bear large white beans; reliable and productive; will grow until frost; pole habit—*80 days (fresh)/95 days (dry)*

Vermont Cranberry (H)—large dark red beans; can be utilized as a fresh or a dried bean; keeps in storage; 6" pods contain 5-6 beans; plants produce reliably and are easy to shell; work well in northern climates with cooler temperatures; bush habit—*60 days (fresh)/90 days (dry)*

Beets—*Beta vulgaris*

Ideal P.H.—6.2-7.0
Feed—light
Light requirements—full sun—will tolerate some shade
Family—Spinach

Friends:

Vegetables: broccoli, Brussels sprouts, cabbage, carrots, cauliflower, chard, kale, kohlrabi, melons, salad greens (like mustard and arugula), and onions
Flowers and Herbs: mint (in a container, of course), beets also fare well with many flowers, pick ones that reach a foot or so in height, like love-in-a-mist or calendula

To Grow:

Beets can be started outside in early spring, as soon as the soil can be worked and the temperatures reach around 50 degrees. Those who live in warmer climates can also start beets 10 to 12 weeks before the frost date for a fall crop.

Insert beet seeds with a dibble 1 inch deep, and space the seeds 3 inches apart. To ensure germination, place burlap over the seedbed and keep the seeds moist

---

FOR COMPANION PLANTING

1. Beets will fare well in a bed with other root crops and salad greens. The salad greens will discourage the growth of weeds (see page 152).

2. They can also be intermixed with brassica family plants during the spring, while the brassicas are still small. Try adding them to a bed of broccoli, Brussels sprouts, or cauliflower, and add some salad greens in the extra space.

1 - Salad Greens
2 - Broccoli
3 - Calendula and Love-in-a-Mist
4 - Beets
5 - Cauliflower

until the seedlings sprout. Each beet seed will sprout several seedlings, so thinning is essential for mature healthy-sized beets. Beet thinnings make a sweet treat in spring salads.

Beets should be mulched to help keep them cool in the spring, and the root tops should be kept covered as they emerge from the soil. Make sure to keep beets well watered as a lack of even moisture will make the roots tough and woody. Beets will become stunted when weeds grow too close by, or even when a gardener tills the surrounding soil, so seed them in a place where they won't be disturbed.

To Harvest:

Beets can be harvested as young seedlings for their greens or as mature roots. Spring beets should be harvested before temperatures reach beyond 85 degrees. In the fall, beets can be harvested after the first frost. Cut the tops from the beets, leaving about one inch of green so that the beets don't bleed and stain. Beets will store in a root cellar over winter.

Foes:

Beets do not have many enemies in the garden. Their leaves are susceptible to flea beetles, so consider planting arugula nearby as a trap crop.

SEED POSSIBILITIES:

Beets grow in colors of deep red, white, orange, and gold. If you find that you don't like the taste of red beets, try the more mild flavored colors of white, gold, and orange for a nutty mild taste.

Chioggia (H)—mild and sweet flavor; reach 2" round; sport concentric circles of deep red and white; beet greens are also edible and tasty—65 days

Detroit Dark Red (H)—reliably generate smooth 3" deep red beets; beet tops grow to 14" in height; keeps well—55-65 days

Early Wonder Tall Top (OP)—grow quickly in early spring; round shape measures 3-4"; greens are tender and mild; grows well in spring or fall—50 days

Broccoli and Cauliflower—*Brassica oleracea, Italica,* and *Botrytis groups* respectively

Ideal P.H.—6.0-7.0
Feed—moderate to heavy
Light requirements—full sun (can tolerate some shade but will produce smaller heads)
Family—Brassica

Friends:

Vegetables and Fruits: bush beans, beets, carrots, cucumbers, lettuce, onions, and other brassicas, including cabbage, collards, kale, and Brussels sprouts
Herbs and Flowers: asters, anise hyssop, calendula, chamomile, dill, marigolds, mint, nasturtiums, parsley, rosemary, sage, thyme, and zinnias

To Grow:

Broccoli and cauliflower plants prefer the cooler temperatures of spring and fall. Most gardeners can produce at least two harvests in a single year. To start from seed, sow seeds 5 to 6 weeks before the frost date.

Seedlings can be transplanted in about 4 weeks, when you see crocuses in bloom.

Both brassicas grow best when temperatures are in the 60s. The plants themselves will grow easily, but they will not produce large heads unless they are planted in rich soil at the start. When transferring seedlings to the outdoor garden, make sure to dig a larger hole than necessary, and then fill that hole with rich compost. Transplants should be spaced about 1½ feet apart from each other on all sides. If the starts have grown leggy, sink the plant in the soil so that the soil surface reaches just below the bottom leaves. Add a barrier around the seedlings to stop cutworms.

Broccoli remains the most popular vegetable of the brassica family, despite the fact that it can be cumbersome to grow. Try brassica family members like kale, collards, or kohlrabi for less laborious alternatives.

Avoid planting when the temperature is still flirting with 40 degrees at night. If broccoli or cauliflower spends too many consecutive nights in temperatures near freezing, it will likely "button," and produce really small heads. Broccoli and cauliflower will also not head well if the soil is calcium deficient. If you've noted a season of growing that resulted in giant plants with no flowers, amend the soil with calcium rich lime before planting the next season. Spray the plants with fish emulsion a month or so after transplant.

To plant seeds for a fall crop of broccoli or cauliflower, make sure to account for a slightly longer growing season. Add on a week or two to the date range on the seed packet. As the temperatures become cooler, "tuck in" your broccoli and cauliflower plants with a nice heavy bed of mulch, like freshly fallen chopped leaves.

To keep the moisture level around broccoli and cauliflower even, make sure to apply some mulch after the transplants are in the ground. Consider planting a living mulch, like sweet asylum or white clover. Both will attract beneficials and indirectly protect brassicas from their many foes.

Mature cauliflower heads turn yellow. Some modern varieties have leaves that fold towards the cauliflower head as the head matures. If you'd prefer to blanch your heads to a more recognizable creamy white hue, once you see a head appearing on the plant, tie the inner leaves over the head with twine.

To Harvest:

Cut about 4 inches down from the floret. Depending on the variety, the plant will continue to produce tinier florets for about 2 weeks, sometimes less, and sometimes more. Sprouting broccoli

Before eating homegrown broccoli or cauliflower, soak the heads in some water with a bit of salt. Any cabbageworms or cabbage loopers that have made the journey inside will float to the surface.

florets can be harvested with their stems. If some of the flowers bloom before you find the chance to harvest the florets, leave the yellow flowers for beneficials.

Foes:

Cabbageworms—Cabbageworms are tiny little green caterpillars that are actually the larvae of the white cabbage butterfly. In their earliest stages, they are often quite minuscule and hide among the veins in the leaves. Most likely, you will spot the damage they create and their black excretions before you find them slinking on the undersides of your brassica leaves. Beneficial insects

FOR COMPANION PLANTING

As broccoli, cauliflower, and other brassicas have many small pests as foes, they really benefit from companion planting techniques that attract beneficial insects and mask the odor of the brassicas. As I've mentioned, planting crops of the same plant family can sometimes lead to a higher level of attacks by pests. I've not found this to be the case with brassicas. In any brassica family bed, try to plant a mix of flowers so that blooming flowers surround the broccoli throughout the growing season.

I grow my broccoli, kohlrabi, cabbage, and cauliflower in the same bed because they all have shorter growing seasons. In midsummer, once the spring brassicas are finished producing, I'll transplant some cucumber starts, or seed a bed for fall carrots and beets. If you have a smaller garden space, you can include all of your brassicas in the same bed.

1. Try planting broccoli and cauliflower in among other brassicas, including kohlrabi or cabbage. Surround the plants with zinnias, calendula, dill, thyme, or a low growing cover crop, like white clover. With the right placement, this bed could grow quite beautifully.

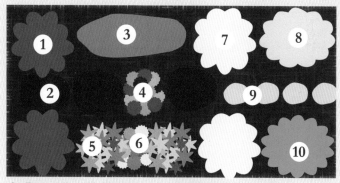

1 - Broccoli	5 - Zinnias	8 - Thyme
2 - Cabbage	6 - Calendulas	9 - Kohlrabi
3 - Dill	7 - Cauliflower	10 - Parsley
4 - Marigolds		

2. Interplant cauliflower and broccoli with white clover and an outer border of zinnias and calendula.

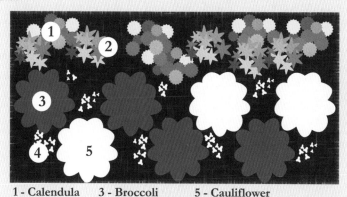

1 - Calendula	3 - Broccoli	5 - Cauliflower
2 - Zinnias	4 - White Clover	

In smaller gardens, divide the bed according to the varying growth rates of the brassicas. That way, brassicas that need a full season for harvest (like Brussels sprouts) won't shade new transplants.

will help in your attempts to combat these little critters, however hand picking is also an option.

Cabbage Loopers—Cabbage loopers are so named because their backs form little loop humps to propel them forward. They are the larvae of a nocturnal gray moth. At 1½ inches long and with a thick diameter, they are much easier to spot than cabbageworms.

Cabbage loopers will chew the leaves of brassica crops, and they will even crawl within the broccoli heads. Just as with cabbageworms, hand picking is possible, and beneficial insects will find them a tasty treat.

Diamondback Moths—The larvae of the diamondback moth also feeds on brassica family members. Although similar in appearance to the cabbageworm

In one scientific study, lettuce, beans, and onions were all intercropped with cauliflower. Each variety of cultivar exhibited a greater rate of production than when grown independently.

and cabbage looper, the diamondback larvae has two back "legs" and is quite tiny (1/5 of an inch). If you rustle the leaves of your brassica plants, these larvae will drop to the ground. There may be more diamondback moths, but they tend to cause less damage than other brassica pests.

These pests seem to leave sprouting varieties of broccoli alone, so try planting *Purple Sprouting* broccoli for a pest resistant alternative. If you find your plants overwhelmed by pests, even after including herbs and flowers within your brassica bed, consider implementing row covers the next season.

SEED POSSIBILITIES:

For Broccoli:
Calabrese (H)—classic broccoli variety that arrived in America with Italian immigrants; generously sized green heads—58-90 days
Purple Sprouting (H)—fantastic cold hardy variety, overwintering (below 10 degrees Fahrenheit); is known for its prolific sprouts in early spring—220 days
Waltham (OP)—large dark blue/green heads; bred to withstand frost; will overwinter in warmer climates—80-85 days

For Cauliflower:
Amazing (OP)—self wrapping leaves; grown in multiple climate zones; fall variety; vigorous—65-75 days
Purple of Sicily (OP)—extremely large heads; bright purple color confuses insects; less maintenance; nutrient rich—90 days
Romanesco (H)—gorgeous spiraled lime green heads; seed in midsummer for a fall harvest in cool weather—75-100 days
Snowball Self Blanching (OP)—leaves wrap around heads to blanch; longstanding favorite; large heads; accommodates to warm weather climate—60-70 days

Brussels Sprouts—*Brassica oleracea (Gemmifera group)*

Ideal P.H.—5.5-6.8
Feed—moderate
Light requirements—full sun to partial shade
Family—brassica

Friends:

Vegetables and Fruits: beets, carrots, cucumbers, onions, and other brassicas, including cabbage, cauliflower, collards, and kale

Herbs and Flowers: calendula, chamomile, dill, geraniums, hyssop, marigolds, mint, nasturtiums, parsley, rosemary, sage, thyme, and zinnias

To Grow:

Seed Brussels sprouts 5 to 6 weeks before the frost date in your area to make sure they have ample time to mature during the growing season.

Brussels sprouts have a much slower growth rate than other members of the brassica family and can take up to four months to produce. I start my seeds indoors to guarantee a sufficient growing

---

FOR COMPANION PLANTING

1. Brussels sprouts and other brassicas really offer an opportunity to design a creative companion planted bed with a multitude of herbs, flowers, and living mulch. Once the Brussels sprouts seedlings have been transferred to the bed, seed some calendula, geraniums, or marigolds around the edges. Tuck some dill or zinnia seeds between the Brussels sprouts, or sprinkle some white clover seeds around the base of the plants. As long as the roots of the Brussels sprouts don't become crowded, feel free to seed with abandon.

1 - Nasturtiums
2 - Brussels Sprouts
3 - White Clover
4 - Onions
5 - Parsley
6 - Geraniums

> Brussels sprouts do take up bunches of space over the long growing season, but they're one of the few crops I can leave in the garden until December, and they're amazingly delicious when cooked with bacon. Because I value my Brussels sprouts so highly, I make up the space by growing lettuce in the shade of the Brussels' broad leaves.

season. Choose their bed placement carefully as they will remain there for most of the garden year. Although Brussels sprouts will grow contently with other brassica family members, I plant mine in a separate space to minimize root disruption. If you have a small garden space, include them in a brassica family bed. Give them about 15 inches of space in all directions.

Brussels sprouts are heavy feeders and will appreciate a fertilizer boost from fish emulsion or aerated compost tea each month.

To Harvest:

During the growing season, buds will gradually begin to form at the base of the plant. Once you see the formation of those lower buds, remove the lowest 6 or 8 leaves from the plant. Remove additional leaves 2 to 3 at a time in successive weeks. Once the lowest buds reach harvesting size, they can be picked from the plant. Buds can be harvested continually throughout the fall. To encourage further maximum bud size, chop off the uppermost portion of the plant leaves while the buds are still small to transfer the plant's energy towards bud formation.

Brussels sprouts will keep in the garden past frost and will taste sweeter even after frost's first nip.

> Some Brussels sprouts will "blow" before they reach maturity. This means that the sprouts open into a flower shape. They are still edible, but their blown shape indicates that the sprouts needed more nutrients during the growing season. Hybrid varieties are less likely to have blown sprouts; I've had good luck with *Roodnerf.*

Foes:

Brussels sprouts attract the same pests as broccoli. See page 140 and 142 for a description of cabbage worms, cabbage loopers, and diamondback moth larvae. Cutworms will cut down the tiny transplants in the middle of the night, so make sure to keep the seedlings protected after outdoor planting. Brussels sprouts require companion flowers and herbs throughout the growing season to ward off potential pests.

SEED POSSIBILITIES:

Roodnerf (OP)—easy to grow; delicious green sprouts; one of the few open pollinated varieties that has shown disease and pest resistance—*100 days*
Nautic (F1)—breed to produce large full sprouts; also resists diseases; stands without support—*120 days*
Catskill (H)—short stout plants, generate heavy stems full of large 1.5-2 inch sprouts—*85-110 days*

Cabbage—*Brassica oleracea (Capitata group)*

Ideal P.H.—6.0-6.8
Feed—moderate
Light requirements—full sun
Family—brassica

Friends:

Vegetables: bush beans, beets, carrots, celery, cucumbers, lettuce, onions, potatoes, spinach, Swiss chard, or members of the brassica family

Flowers and Herbs: asters, borage, chamomile, clover, dill, hyssop, nasturtium, rosemary, sage, southernwood, thyme, and most aromatic herbs

To Grow:

Cabbage can be grown in both the spring and fall in most climates. To produce a crop for spring, start seedlings indoors 6 to 8 weeks before your last frost date. Cabbage plants are particular about temperature. Try to find a point in your growing season where temperatures are even and moderately warm—between 60 and 75 degrees during the day, and not below 45 to 50 degrees at night.

FOR COMPANION PLANTING

As with other brassicas, companion planting allows gardeners to bury, or mask, the smell of cabbage by planting the cabbage among strongly scented herbs and flowers. A study indicated that when cabbage was intercropped with white clover, populations of predatory insects rose dramatically. Include borage, dill, or any other low growing flowers and herbs that you might have on hand with your brassicas.

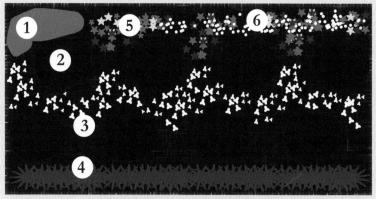

1 - Dill	3 - White Clover	5 - Borage
2 - Cabbage	4 - Onions	6 - Chamomile

If you'd like to include edibles with your cabbage plants, add onions along the edges, and plant carrots, celery, lettuce, or spinach on the southern side.

See page 141 for an interplanted brassica bed.

Once the temperature reaches that point, your cabbage starts can be transplanted outside. Give each cabbage plant at least a foot of space on all sides.

Like other brassicas, cabbage feeds heavily from rich soil and needs a rich shovel of compost at planting. Spray cabbage plants with some fish emulsion to give them a boost of nutrients midway through the season, and add some mulch around the cabbage to moderate the soil moisture.

To Harvest:

As the cabbage plant forms heads, cut away rotten leaves. Remove the main head with a knife, and let the rest of the plant stay in the garden for a few more weeks. The cabbage will grow smaller cabbage heads. Fall cabbage should be harvested before first frost.

Foes:

Cabbage might have the longest list of named foes in the garden out of all the edibles. Anyone who reads about the growing of cabbage might be alarmed by the description of possible issues. I don't believe that cabbage is really that more susceptible to attack than other plants in the garden. Cabbage was one of the most important crops in colonial times. It was used to feed livestock, and it was among the main list of foods for many colonial residents. Perhaps its legacy as a food of relative importance made gardeners take more notice of any pests?

At any rate, there are cabbageworms, cabbage loopers, and diamondback moths (all are discussed on pages 140 and 142), and there are cabbage maggots. Cabbage maggot invasions can be prevented with floating row covers and crop rotation. Red and savoy varieties are less commonly attacked, so if your cabbage has suffered through a "holy" season, try red or savoy cabbage instead.

> Although holey cabbage leaves are unsightly, they can still be eaten. I've never really noticed a difference in taste.

SEED POSSIBILITIES:

Caraflex (F1)—savoy variety; compact pointed heads with crisp leaves; can be utilized in container plantings because they only reach 10-14" in spread; perfect for spring or fall—*68 days*

Copenhagen Market (OP)—compact variety; heads measure 6-8" and generally weigh 3-5 lbs.; plants extend 25" in width; grows well in many climates—*65-100 days*

Gonzales (F1)—a "baby cabbage" with miniature sized heads that measure 4-6" in width and weigh only 3 lbs.; these cabbages are perfect for the small gardener; work well in raised beds—*66 days*

Red Acre (OP)—produces bright, compact reddish purple heads; a great variety for small gardens; can replace spring crops for a fall harvest; keeps really well in storage—*75 days*

Super Red (F1)—moderately sized (3-5 lbs.) dark red heads; lovely flavor with a hint of pepper; excellent in a variety of dishes—*80 days*

Carrots—*Daucus carota*

Ideal P.H.—6.5
Feed—light feeder
Light requirements—full sun
Family—parsley

Friends:

Vegetables: beets, lettuce, onions, peas, peppers, radishes, and tomatoes
Herbs and Flowers: caraway, calendulas, chamomile, chives, love-in-a-mist, rosemary, and sage

To Grow:

Carrots prefer soil that is loose and free from rocks or other debris. They grow to a bigger size, and with better flavor, if a healthy dose of compost is added to the soil before the seeds are planted. They can be sown early in spring, and several successions can be planted throughout the summer. Rocks will prevent carrots from growing long and straight and can stunt the carrots altogether.

Carrot seeds need light to germinate, but the seeds can blow away with the wind if they're not held down. After laying down the seeds on the soil surface, place some burlap over as a cover, spray the burlap lightly with a hose, and add some rocks to the edges to keep the burlap in place. The burlap will let in enough light to allow germination, but it will prevent the seeds from fluttering away on a windy day. Check for seedlings every few days, and remove the burlap once a clear line of seedlings sprout. The seedlings are fairly tiny, so make sure to look closely!

Make sure to thin the carrots as they grow. It can be painful to pull out the little seedlings, but overcrowded carrots will grow irregularly or become stunted without the necessary thinning. Once the carrots have become established, provide a fine mulch of grass clippings between the rows.

> Originally, the first carrots that were used were actually purple. References to them first show up in Spain around 950 C.E. The common carrot became yellow in the 16th century and wasn't actually orange until the 18th century.

To Harvest:

As carrots grow towards maturity, little carrot tops will sprout from the ground. Cover the tops with a little soil or mulch until you think they're large enough to pull. This will prevent the tops from turning green. Watering the soil when harvesting, or loosening with a digging fork can help to break up the soil before the carrots are removed. Avoid pulling carrots from tight compact soil as the carrots can and will snap.

Leave a couple carrots in the garden over winter. In the spring, they'll produce little flower heads that will attract beneficial hoverflies and wasps to the garden.

Carrots can be harvested on an "as needed" basis by the kitchen gardener, but make sure to cover them with at least a foot of mulch before the ground freezes in colder climates.

FOR COMPANION PLANTING

Carrots provide easy companion planting options. When planting, intermix the seeds with radish seeds. Radishes grow within a month and will be pulled from the patch shortly after. By mixing the radish seeds in with the carrots, you can thin the carrots automatically. The radishes will also help if the soil is compacted by rain. Radish sprouts are much stronger than carrot sprouts, and they will loosen the soil for the carrots.

1. Interplant rows of carrots in a bed with beets, onions, and lettuce.

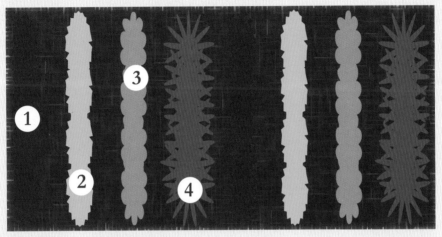

1 - Beets   3 - Carrots
2 - Lettuce   4 - Onions

2. Carrots can also be interplanted within a bed of lettuce, peas, and a variety of flowers and herbs.

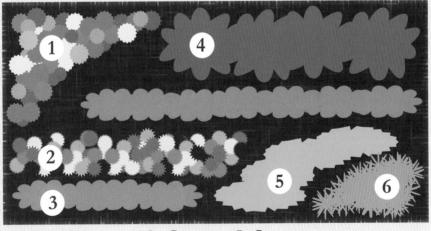

1 - Calendula   3 - Carrots   5 - Lettuce
2 - Love-in-a-Mist   4 - Peas   6 - Sage

Foes:

The Carrot Rust Fly—The carrot rust fly, a tiny insect measuring 1/5 of an inch, will lay its eggs in the crown of the plant. The larvae of the carrot rust fly attack by chewing tunnels along the exterior of the root and leaving a brownish excretion. Although carrot rust flies are most likely to appear in northwest gardens, their damage has been documented throughout most of North America.

Scientific studies have indicated that intercropping does decrease the appearance of the carrot rust fly. The flies find carrots by smell, so aromatic plants, like marigolds, onions, and rosemary, all led to a reduced rate of infestation.

Studies have indicated that dill, anise, and parsnips all stunt the growth of carrots, so avoid planting them nearby.

SEED POSSIBILITIES:

In our garden, we plant a variety of hues. The texture and flavor of each varies as much as the color. Plant a few varieties to see which best suit your soil.

Cosmic Purple (OP)—brilliant purple tone with yellow and orange centers—*70 days*
Danvers (H)—deep orange carrots with thick roots—*70 days*
Red Cored Chantenay (H)—orange exterior and red interior; turns sweeter in storage—*65 days*
Scarlet Nantes (OP)—straight uniform orange carrots that are sweet to the center—*65 days*
Yellowstone (H)—light yellow carrots; prolific; mild sweet flavor—*70 days*
White Satin (H)—a classically colored carrot; sweet and mild—*68 days*

Celery—*Apium graveolens*

Ideal P.H.—6.5-7.0
Feed—heavy
Light requirements—full sun to light shade
Family—carrot

Friends:

Vegetables: beans, cabbage, cauliflower, collards, kale, leeks, and potatoes
Flowers and Herbs: Most all herbs and flowers flourish with celery nearby—try love-in-a-mist, calendula, cosmos, or zinnias.

FOR COMPANION PLANTING

Celery makes friends with most edibles in the garden and isn't picky about its placement. Celery can be planted in a bed with beans and potatoes (see page 197). It will also grow contently with tomatoes, or with brassicas like cauliflower, cabbage, kale, or collards. Squeeze a plant or two on the edges of a carrot and onion bed.

To Grow:

Celery requires a bit more attention than the average vegetable because the plant requires blanching and an extended growing season. Seedlings should be started indoors, about 10 to 12 weeks before the last frost. It's a bit tricky to get celery seeds to germinate. I've found that a seed-starting mat isn't necessary—the seeds prefer temperatures between 60 and 70 degrees. Soak the seeds overnight to increase the prospect of germination and seed thickly. It can take 2 to 3 weeks for seedlings to appear.

Once celery seedlings reach 2 inches in height, they should be transferred to larger containers. Transplants should be set in the ground when the danger of frost has passed and nighttime temperatures have reached at least 55 degrees. Transplants should be set approximately 8 to 10 inches apart.

If you'd like just a little bit of celery in your life, try growing cutting celery. Cutting celery grows more like an herb, with pencil thin stalks and a mass of leaves at the top. Cutting celery also doesn't require blanching or a vigilant watering schedule. Try a variety like Afina, and plant with a floral border for a flush of green. If you live in zone 5 or above, leave it in the ground. It will reseed voluntarily year after year.

To grow large healthy plants, celery requires steady watering (1 inch a week) and fertilizer boost (like fish emulsion) once every two weeks. Blanching celery stalks will encourage a milder flavor. I blanch my plants by pulling up soil around the plant during the growing season, and then wrap them in newspaper towards the season's end. To wrap the plants a few weeks before harvest, I bunch the plant together like a bouquet and tie some newspaper around the base of the plant with twine.

To Harvest:

Celery can be harvested a stalk at a time during the growing season, or the whole plant can be cut at the root once it reaches its final size.

Another form of celery has recently been making the rounds in CSA boxes and confusing diligent cooks throughout the country. Celeriac has a knobby mangled exterior and white flesh with a mild nutty celery taste inside. It stores really well in a cool root cellar, so it's a wintery alternative for celery flavor.

Foes:

Celery doesn't have too many pests. I've noticed a few swallowtail butterfly caterpillars on mine, but I let them stay.

SEED POSSIBILITIES:

Red Venture (H)—stalks of red with green foliage; less common intense celery flavor; cold hardy—*100-110 days*

Tango (F1)—grows well in many climates, but better in northern latitudes; vigorous grower; stalks reach between 18-20"; tender and sweet, some to be left to flower for seeds—*85 days*

Corn—*Zea mays*

Ideal P.H.—5.5-6.8
Feed—heavy
Light requirements—full
Family—grass

Friends:

Vegetables and Fruits: pole beans, bush or vine squash, also, cucumbers, melons or pumpkins, parsnips, peas, potatoes, and members of the brassica family
Flowers: sunflowers and nasturtiums

To Grow:

To cultivate strong sturdy corn, you really need to start with a garden bed that is rich in compost and not weed seeds. Corn does not survive frost, so seeds should be planted once the soil has warmed to 60 degrees, and the danger of frost has passed.

Depending on the style of companion planting you chose, use a dibble to plant the corn, or dig a trench about 4 inches deep. Cover the seeds with an inch of soil and a gentle douse of water. As the seeds germinate and begin to grow, gradually add soil around the seedlings until the soil is level with the surrounding ground. Whether the seeds are planted in mounds or trenches, each seed should be separated by at least 10 inches of space. Space each row 2½ feet apart, and make sure to plant a block of corn. Corn is pollinated by the wind. Each little corn silk is attached to a kernel of corn, and each must be pollinated for that kernel to grow. As a result, it is best to plant corn in a block of at least 4 rows to ensure abundant pollination.

As heavy feeders, corn seedlings benefit from a douse of fish emulsion a month into the growing season.

The germination rate of corn seeds will drop off sharply in the second year. To use up old seed, put 2 or 3 seeds in the same hole instead of just one. Snip the extra sprouts with scissors.

To Harvest:

Fresh corn can be tricky to harvest if you're not aware of some telltale signs. As the ears of corn reach maturity, the corn silk will turn brown, and the cob will become more rounded towards bottom. Kernels that are ready for eating have a white milky interior. Try shucking a small section of the corn ear and piercing a kernel to check. If the corn looks ready, stick it in a pot of boiling water or on your grill as quickly as possible. The fresher the corn, the sweeter its taste will be. If you'd like to dry your corn for seed or for storage, leave the cobs of corn on the stalk for 6 to 8 more weeks.

As long as the leftover vines and stalks are weed and pest free, they can be added to a compost pile or chopped down to compost right in the plant bed.

FOR COMPANION PLANTING

The most classic combination in companion planting is the "three sisters" bed. Native Americans throughout North America planted beans, squash, and corn in the same area, as they found the combination of the three to be mutually beneficial. The beans produced nitrogen and encouraged the growth of the corn. The corn acted as a trellis for the beans to climb, and the beans helped to stabilize the corn's placement in the ground. The squash plants rambled along the ground and provided ground cover. As a living mulch, the squash also discouraged the growth of weeds and helped to retain moisture within the soil.

More recent scientific studies have verified what Native Americans have known all along. One study noted that interplanting beans with corn reduced the number of pests on both. Another study verified the impact of the legume's nitrogen with the soil. When the beans were planted around the corn, the corn's yield increased.

The type of "three sisters" bed that is best for your garden may depend upon the amount of natural rainfall in your climate. In our area of the northeast, I've always planted my corn and beans in mounds, in the tradition of the Wampanoag Indians. For those who live in the drier climate of the southwest, it is better to set up the bed with small trenches, like the Zuni Indians.

One of the essential steps for success with a "three sisters bed" is timing. The corn and squash should be planted first, before the beans. The beans should be added to the plot once the corn seedlings reach 3 to 4 inches in height. Pick pole bean varieties that indicate a longer growing season so that they grow with the corn and don't overtake the corn as it grows. Although the squash plants will eventually provide ground cover, the soil will need mulch before the squash vines attain their dominance over the area. If you've decided to plant a "three sisters" garden, you'll need to create a double wide (at least 10x10) garden bed to promote proper pollination.

Kitchen gardeners often have less space available in the garden and can't accommodate a full-sized "three sisters" bed. To plant a mini-sized "three sisters" bed, try incorporating bush squash instead of vining squash. Because the bush squash won't have rambling vines, they won't overwhelm the bed, and they won't need as much room.

If you'd like to eliminate the squash completely, try planting the corn in a block with pole beans and lettuce and nasturtiums or clover. The lettuce, nasturtiums, or clover will provide some ground cover until the beans and corn reach maturity. Remember, plant the beans after the corn reaches 3 to 4 inches in height.

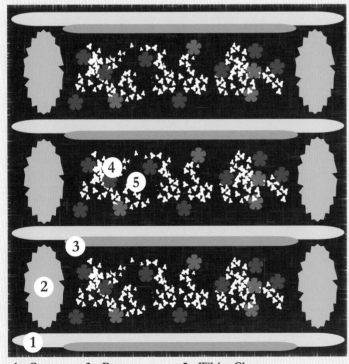

1 - Corn   3 - Beans   5 - White Clover
2 - Lettuce   4 - Nasturtiums

The "three sisters method" is always mentioned as the touchstone of companion planting. Unfortunately, many gardening books fail to mention that Native Americans mostly grew corn and beans for drying. I wouldn't suggest planting sweet corn or beans for fresh eating in a "three sisters" bed. The logistics involve tramping within a thickly planted bed over prickly squash vines to reach the beans and corn. It just doesn't make sense for a kitchen gardener constrained by space.

If you'd like to plant a Native American style "three sisters" bed, make sure to refer to *Native American Gardening*, by Michael Caduto and Joseph Bruchac. They outline several variations of the "three sisters" beds; each incorporates Native American tradition and is specialized for regional climates.

the larvae hatch, they will eat pathways through the corn kernels, particularly towards the top. European corn borers inflict similar damage.

Predatory insects, birds, and bats will all eat corn earworms during the season. The larvae can overwinter in the soil in climates zone 6 and higher, so be sure to clear any corn debris from the garden if you've spotted their damage. Corn earworms are named for their particular affection for corn, however, they've also been known to attack cotton, tomatoes, beans, and peppers.

Even if the corn earworms inflict some damage on your crop, much of the ear of the corn is often still salvageable. If you have chickens, they'd bawk in appreciation over an ear top garnished with corn earworms.

Foes:

The Corn Earworm—Corn earworms are fat brownish caterpillars that are the larvae of a moth. They measure about an inch in length; however, they can grow up to 1½ inches. The moths will lay their eggs on the tops of corn ears, and when

SEED POSSIBILITIES:

Because of corn's wind pollination, it can be challenging to grow more than one variety in a single garden space. If you'd really like to grow two or more varieties, try to create some type of wind barrier. Use tall flowers, like sunflowers, in between any sections of corn. Or, try planting a variety in a front flowerbed. Strains of corn have been adapted for fresh eating, for flour, popcorn, and as ornamentals. Even though I've included some popular national favorites here, make sure to check with your local Cooperative Extension, or with local organic farmers, to see which varieties are known for local success.

Note: Each year, it has become increasingly challenging to find corn that does not test positive for genetic modification. Seek out companies that test their corn seed for GMO contamination on a yearly basis.

For sweet corn:

Luscious (F1)—super sweet buttery flavor; grows well in northern climates—*75 days*

Country Gentleman (H)—white sweet corn; beautiful shoepeg pattern (corn does not grow in rows)—*90 days*

Golden Bantam (H)—a classic sweet corn, grown for over 100 years—*78 days*

For dried corn:

Cherokee White Eagle (H)—dent corn meant for drying; blue and white kernels; legend tells of its journey with the Cherokee on the Trail of Tears—*110 days*

Hopi Blue Corn (H)—traditional blue corn of the Hopi Indians; dual purpose, can be eaten fresh if harvested early; grows well in the Southwest—*85-105 days*

Strawberry Popcorn—dark red kernels; 2" ears, stalks grow only 3' with 2-4 ears per stalk; perfect for small gardens—*100 days*

Cucumbers—*Cucumis sativus*

Ideal P.H.—6.5
Feed—heavy
Light requirements—full sun
Family—Cucurbit

Friends:

Vegetables and Fruits: beans, cabbage, corn, lettuce, peas, radishes, and spinach
Flowers and Herbs: basil, dill, marigolds, nasturtiums, pansies, red clover, and sunflowers

To Grow:

Cucumber should be seeded in hills measuring approximately 1 foot in diameter approximately 2 to 3 weeks after the last frost date. Add about 6 to 8 seeds per hill at a depth of 2 inches. Once the plants sprout, thin the seedlings to 4 sprouts per hill. If the vines have been left to sprawl, leave 3 to 4 feet between hills. If you've included a trellis, 2 feet of space between hills is sufficient.

To prevent water distress, mulch around the seedlings towards the beginning of the growing season. Cucumbers that have experienced uneven watering, or insufficient watering, will often taste bitter.

If you've noticed an issue with powdery mildew in the past, try starting your cucumber seedlings indoors. Powdery mildew tends to strike in the later part of the summer. By giving the plants a head start, the mildew might strike after the vines have generated an ample supply of fruit for the season.

As the cucumber plants reach the peak of production, the vines will sprawl every which way and will take down any plants within the vicinity. Once the plants reach the edge of the bed, or the top of the trellis, nip the ends of the vines to discourage excessive growth. The vines will turn their energy towards cucumber production.

FOR COMPANION PLANTING

1. Cucumbers are quite compatible with members of the cabbage family, particularly spring broccoli and cabbage. Radishes, carrots, and peas also pair well in a companion planted bed. A scientific study noted a reduced amount of cucumber beetles when the cucumber vines were interplanted with broccoli; another study indicated a similar benefit with radishes. After the spring broccoli is pulled, plant peas or beans in the freed space to replenish the soil.

1 - Radishes   3 - Cucumbers   5 - Spinach
2 - Basil   4 - Broccoli   6 - Nasturtiums

2. Cucumbers can also be interplanted with peas, carrots, and radishes. The radishes, carrots, and peas can be replaced by lettuce and spinach in early fall.

    Although cucumber vines can certainly sprawl along the ground, I'd suggest adding a trellis. Allowing the cucumbers to grow above the soil will increase airflow. In case the cucumber vines develop powdery mildew, the chance of the disease spreading among the vines will diminish.

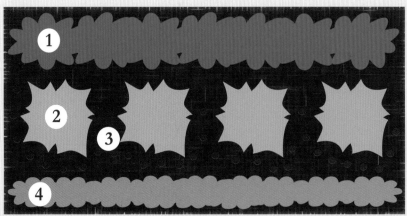

1 - Peas   3 - Radishes
2 - Cucumbers 4 - Carrots

3. Cucumbers, corn, beans, nasturtiums, and marigolds could also be considered for interplanting in a modified "three sisters" bed. (See the example on page 158, and replace some of the white clover and nasturtiums with cucumber plants.)

To Harvest:

Once the plants start yielding harvestable fruit, they will grow quickly and should be harvested at least every other day. Cucumbers like to hide under their leaves and can grow to a tremendous size if not found. Depending on the variety, most cucumbers taste best when harvested at a length of 3 to 4 inches. If they grow much larger, they will become bitter and seedy.

Foes:

The Cucumber Beetle—Cucumber beetles measure approximately 1/4 of an inch in length, and they have distinctive black and yellow stripes on their backs. They will eat the leaves, vines, flowers, and the cucumbers themselves. To reduce their population, you can hand pick them as you see them appear, and the plants can be protected by floating row covers if necessary.

Cucumber beetles tend to attack the garden at a certain point in the summer. If you've seen cucumber beetles in your garden in the past, try planting several successions of plants, instead of all at once. One of the successions is bound to miss the beetle's arrival.

Companion gardeners have noticed that potatoes and cucumbers do not grow well together. Cucumbers will weaken the potatoes' defense system against blight. Companion planting tradition also suggests that cucumbers should not be planted with aromatic herbs, like thyme, oregano, or sage.

> The gherkin, the cucumber variety beloved by picklers and hipsters, was first distinguished as an individual variety in the West Indies. Somehow, during the years of the slave trade, the gherkin made its way from Africa to Jamaica.

SEED POSSIBILITIES:

Cool Breeze (FI)—French cornichon; pickling variety; crunchy and fresh tasting—*45 days*
Bushy (H)—classic pickling cucumber; also tasty when eaten fresh—*45-50 days*
Mexican Sour Gherkins/Mouse Melons (H)—bite-sized cucumbers with a hint of lemon flavor; prolific; require trellising—*75 days*
Miniature White (H)—light, sweet, and mild flavor, best if picked while less than 3", vines only reach 3' in length; suitable for trellises and small gardens—*50-55 days*

Eggplants—*Solanum melongena*

Ideal P.H.—6.5
Feed—heavy
Light requirements—full sun
Family—nightshade

Friends:

Vegetables: bush beans, salad greens, peppers, and tomatoes
Herbs and Flowers: basil, dill, marigolds, tarragon, and thyme

FOR COMPANION PLANTING

1. Eggplants, peppers, and basil will grow nicely in a bed interplanted with marigolds. Incorporate some salad greens into the bed early in the season while the eggplants and peppers are still small.

1 - Marigolds   3 - Spinach   5 - Eggplant
2 - Basil   4 - Pepper

2. Eggplants could also be interplanted with bush beans, basil, and marigolds.

1 - Bush Beans   3 - Basil
2 - Marigolds   4 - Eggplant

To Grow:

Eggplants like warm weather and won't fare well if placed in the garden too early. Most gardeners will find it helpful to start the seeds indoors 6 to 8 weeks before their last frost date. Spring wind and rain will cause the plants to stagnate, so delay transplant until the weather has moderated to summerlike conditions (at least 2 weeks past the frost date for your area). Each plant should be allowed a foot and a half of space on either side.

Eggplants are heavy feeders, and should be planted with compost, and then side dressed with mulch during the season. Give each plant a little over a foot of space when transplanted.

To Harvest:

Pick eggplants when they reach an adult size, and their skin has become shiny and smooth. Regular picking will encourage further production.

Foes:

The Flea Beetle—Eggplants can be damaged by an infestation of flea beetles. Flea beetles are extremely small and will only appear as little dots on the eggplants' leaves. If you suspect flea beetle damage, try shaking the plant leaves a little. The beetles will form a mini dust cloud when disturbed.

Flea beetle damage is minimal when eggplants are companion planted. Aromatic flowers and herbs will protect eggplants from substantial devastation. Crimson clover was also shown to have an impact in a scientific study.

Eggplants don't seem to have any obvious enemies; however, the plants will fare better if they are protected from damage by their companion plants.

SEED POSSIBILITIES:

Black Beauty (H)—large bell-shaped dark plum fruits; longer growing season—*90 days*
Listada di Gandia (H)—gorgeous purple striped Italian variety; very productive; petite size, fit in your palm; tasty—*85 days*
Ophelia (F1)—tiny fruits, approximately egg-sized; deep purple in color; plants reach a mere 2' in height; grows well in containers—*55 days*
Ping Tong Long (H)—highly productive; stake for peak performance; dark purple in color; long skinny fruits (12" long and 2" wide)—*60-70 days*
Rosita (H)—lavender and pink fruits; mildly flavored; 6-8" in length and 4-6" in width—*70-80 days*

Garlic—*Allium sativum*

Ideal P.H.—6.5
Feed—heavy
Light requirements—full sun
Family—allium

Friends:

Vegetables: many vegetables, including tomatoes, eggplants, peppers, and brassica family plants

---

FOR COMPANION PLANTING
Garlic should really be spread throughout many beds in the garden (except beds with legumes) as its pungent smell will mask the scent of other annuals and hide them from pests. See examples on pages 185 and 219.

To Grow:

Growing garlic appears daunting to many first time gardeners because in most climates, garlic is planted in the fall. This concern is unwarranted, however, because garlic is one of the easiest annuals you can add to your garden.

Garlic should be planted around Columbus Day (later in the South), in a bed that has been freshened with some fall compost. Divide the heads into single bulbs, and be careful not to strip the bulbs of their protective outer layers. Each bulb should be placed 3 inches into the soil—use a dibble to approximate depth. Give each bulb 4 to 6 inches of space when planting.

Garlic shoots are one of the first annuals to produce shoots in the spring. As they reach maturity, some bulbs will sprout a singular flower called a scape from the center of the plant. The scapes should be cut from the plant before they begin to flower. The scapes possess a light garlic flavor and are quite tasty in an early spring stir-fry.

To Harvest:

Garlic is ready to harvest in mid to late summer when the lower leaves turn yellow. Gently loosen the soil around the bulbs

> For early season garlic, pull a few bulbs while the stalks are still green. The stalk and the bulb are both edible and more mild than fully mature garlic.

with a pitchfork. Hoist the bulbs from the soil by grasping the garlic near the base of the neck. Once the garlic has been harvested, tie the bulbs together in groups with twine and hang in a shady, warm area to dry and cure.

Give the garlic bulbs a few weeks to cure, then cut the stems from the bulb, trim the roots, and store in a cool dry place for the winter. Though some garlic varieties are reputed to keep better in long-term storage, I haven't really had trouble with any of my garlic as long as it's been kept cool and dry.

Foes:

Garlic doesn't really have any foes of its own. It will stunt legumes, so don't plant it in a bed that will contain peas or beans.

SEED POSSIBILITIES:

Garlic can be divided into hardneck and softneck varieties. Hardneck varieties will grow flower scapes, and softneck varieties won't. Softneck varieties can be braided at the end of the season for storage and often produce better in southern climates.

Hardneck:

Chesnok Red—purple striped late season variety; average 9-10 cloves per bulb; they're cold hardy but will tolerate many climate zones—origin is Shvelisi, Georgia

Elephant—oversized cloves, barely fit in the palm of your hand, weigh 1/2 lb. or more; related to leeks; mildly favored; shorter-term storage

Killarney Red—grows well in wet soil, strongly flavored, 8-10 cloves per bulb, peel separates from clove easily

Music—a popular variety that averages 4-5 generously sized cloves per bulb, it's very cold tolerant, and the bulbs will keep for up to a year

Spanish Roja—commonly known as green garlic; midseason variety is popular among many growers for its flavor; it prefers a cold climate for growing, stores for 4 to 6 months

Softneck:

Early Red Italian—grows well in many regions; can harvest early; lightly flavored; stores well over winter

Inchelium Red—eager and productive throughout the country; layered garlic cloves like an artichoke; 12-20 cloves per bulb; stores 6-9 months

Lorz Italian—possesses a spicy kick of gorgeous flavor; grows well in hot climates; 16 cloves per bulb; stores 6-8 months

Nootka Rose—a late season variety; markedly strong flavor; 5-24 cloves per bulb

Kale and Collards—*Brassica oleracea (Acephala group)*

Ideal P.H.—6.0-7.0
Feed—heavy
Light requirements—full sun
Family—brassica

Friends:

Vegetables: beans, beets, celery, cucumbers, leeks, onions, peas, salad greens, Swiss chard, and other members of the brassica family
Flowers and Herbs: dill, calendula, chamomile, marigolds, and nasturtiums

To Grow:

In most locations, kale and collards can be started outside in early spring, while the crocuses bloom. Sow the seeds 1/2 inch deep. If you'd like to start yours inside, try to seed them around 6 weeks before the frost date in your area. Kale grows tall and lanky, so give it 15 inches of space on all sides when transplanted. Plant some marigolds or calendulas within the allotted space. Collards like a bit more room, 18 inches or so of circumference should suffice.

Collards and kale especially appreciate nutrient rich soil; add some compost to its legs during the season, and spray with fish emulsion once a month or so.

The easiest brassica to grow is undoubtedly kohlrabi. Kohlrabi can fit into smaller spaces than other brassicas, and it reaches maturity rapidly—usually around 10 weeks. Directly seed in the garden a month before the last frost (1/4 of an inch deep) or in early summer for a fall crop. Space seedlings at least 5 inches apart. Like other brassicas, kohlrabi are heavy feeders and love rich soil and a boost from fish emulsion as they grow. In warmer climates (zones 6 and higher), leave kohlrabi in the garden through winter and harvest gradually.

Kohlrabi grows well with beets, celery, cucumbers, salad greens, tomatoes, and nasturtiums. (See page 141 for an example.)

To Harvest:

Both kale and collards taste better after a few light frosts. Plants naturally build frost protection by transforming starch into sugar. Harvest a few leaves in late summer, and gradually harvest a few from each plant towards fall. Pick from the middling leaves, and leave the top shoots. Kale will last through cold winters with little protection, while collards involve a bit more attention.

Foes:

Both kale and collards face attack from the same foes as their brassica brethren—see page 140 and 142 for common brassica foes.

> In all but the most bitter winters, kale will survive until spring. In early spring, tender green shoots will form along the sides. Kales are biennial, so uproot them before they flower unless you'd like to collect the seeds.

FOR COMPANION PLANTING

I like to mix my collards and kale in the same bed. A study showed that when collards were interplanted with bush beans, the beans and the collards both had more parasitic wasps. Add Swiss chard, celery, salad greens, and other flowers and herbs in the available edges.

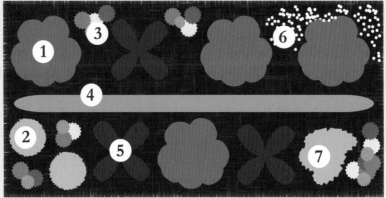

1 - Collards   3 - Calendula   5 - Kale   7 - Salad Greens
2 - Celery   4 - Bush Beans   6 - Chamomile

SEED POSSIBILITIES:

Collards:

Champion (OP)—an all around great variety—resists bolting; hardy in cold; grows well in spring; dark blue/green wavy leaves; plants reach 30" in height—*60-75 days*

Georgia Southern/Georgia Green (H)—mild, tender, juicy leaves; grows well in many climates; slow to bolt; grows well in sandy soil—*60-80 days*

Kale:

Couve Tronchuda/Portuguese Kale (H)—heat tolerant; flat leaves; tastes more like cabbage; ribs of leaves are also edible; reaches 18" in height—*50-60 days*

Lacinato/Dinosaur (H)—dark blue/green textured leaves; grows upright; very cold hardy; flavor is sweeter after frost; reaches 2-3' tall—*60 days*

Winterbor (F1)—known for its winter hardiness; blue-green leaves; reaches 2'; sweet mild flavor; wonderful late fall kale variety—*60 days*

Leeks—*Allium porrum*

Ideal P.H.– 6.0-7.0
Feed—light
Light requirements—full sun to light shade
   (in warmer climates, leeks will prefer a greater amount of shade)
Family—allium

Friends:

In regards to companion planting, leeks should be treated like onions. The spacing may be different, but regard leeks more for their protective qualities. Leeks don't have many pests of their own.

FOR COMPANION PLANTING
See page 194 and page 219 for some examples of companion planted leeks.

To Grow:

If planting from seed, leeks should be started indoors at the same point as onion seedlings (10 to 12 weeks before your last frost date). Like onions, leek seeds can be broadcast over a large tray of potting soil.

When it comes time to plant the leeks outdoors the soil plot will require a little extra preparation. In order to blanch the leeks properly, they need to be planted in trenches. Initially, dig a trench about 6 inches deep. Remove each leek from the soil, and carefully pull the roots so that each seedling is root bare. Stand the leek upright in the trench, and fill dirt around each seedling up to the point where the leaves separate. Give each leek 4 inches of space within the row. As the leeks grow, fill the soil around the base to ensure that the stems are blanched properly. Honestly, if this seems like too much work, just plant your leeks in the same way you would onions. The blanched root might not reach the same length, but you will still cultivate a viable leek.

To Harvest:

Leeks can be harvested as soon as they reach a practical size. If you mulch leeks in the fall with several inches of chopped leaves, they won't freeze, and they can be harvested during the winter.

Even without protection leeks will stay through the winter and can be harvested once the ground thaws in the spring. Leave a few to flower in springtime (they will flower in the fall in southern climates) to attract honeybees.

Foes:

Like other alliums, leeks should not be planted with any member of the legume family. They are not susceptible to attacks from pests.

SEED POSSIBILITIES:

Leeks can be divided into two categories—summer varieties and overwintering varieties. As the names indicate, overwintering varieties are hardier and will last in the garden through colder temperatures.

Summer Varieties:

King Richard (H)—slender stalks; grows upright; pull after the first light frost; one the fastest growing varieties—*75 days*

Megatron (F1)—prolific; should be planted in spring and harvested in early fall; unlikely to bolt in warm weather; nice white shafts—*90 days*

Overwintering Varieties:

Blue Solaise (H)—dependable; pretty deep blue/green leaves; sweet flavor; shafts reach 25-20"; can be grown in northern climates and overwintered—*100-120 days*

Giant Musselburgh (H)—variety reaches 9-15" long; stout stalks—2-3" wide; tender and mild flavor; winter hardy—*80-150 days*

Lancelot (OP)—fast growing; reliable; not dependent on the hours of daylight; shafts reach 12-14"; blanch for longer roots—*95 days*

Melons

Muskmelons—*Cucumis melo*
Watermelons—*Citrullus lanatus*

Ideal P.H.—6.0-6.5
Feed—heavy
Light requirements—full sun
Family—cucurbit

Friends:

Vegetables: corn, peas, radishes, and beets
Flowers and Herbs: nasturtiums, sunflowers, and marigolds

To Grow:

Melons have developed a reputation over the centuries for being particularly tricky to cultivate in the home garden. With a long growing season, melons require more attention and care in northern climates.

Melon seeds should be sown when the soil temperature reaches 65 to 70 degrees 1/2 of an inch deep. For cooler climates, plant several seeds in a larger pot indoors, and transplant when the soil warms. Follow the directions on your seed packet to gauge the number of weeks needed indoors before transplanting. Melon seeds create large seedlings, so it's better not to use small individual seed trays. Once

During the colonial era, some colonists would actually place small melons in their pocket to act as a sort of perfume. Rightfully so, a particular variety of melon earned the name "pocket melon."

Many gardeners develop complex systems for supporting hanging melons as they grow. I've seen quite a few melons hung with pantyhose protectors. In my experience, I've found that the vine will create its own support for the melon. Melons buried among the leaves can rot if they spend too much time in moist soil, so slip a board, plate, or small pot under the melon as it reaches maturity.

Cucurbits form two different sets of flowers—distinguished as "male" and "female." Male flowers will grow about 10 days before the female flowers appear.

FOR COMPANION PLANTING

1. Consider a modified "three sisters" bed interplanted with corn, melons, and nasturtiums. Radishes and greens can fill the bed in the early part of the season, and the melon will overtake the space during the season. (See an example on pg. 158 and replace the nasturtiums with melon plants.)
2. In a kitchen garden, melons might be trellised to save space and to maximize airflow. Consider creating a melon archway over the garden entrance, over a pathway within the garden, or over a singular bed. Surround the base with flowering radishes, marigolds, or nasturtiums.

1 - Radishes
2 - Melons
3 - Nasturtiums
4. Marigolds

three leaves have sprouted, pinch back the tops of the plants. This will encourage the plant to generate multiple shoots instead of one singular vine.

The seeds or seedlings should be planted in small hills (plant 3-5 in each hill). The plants prefer well-drained soil and do not perform well in soggy conditions. It is better to water around the base of the hill and not directly on the crown. Melons are also heavy feeders and will benefit from a douse of fish emulsion or comfrey tea every few weeks or a bit of bone meal tucked in around the base.

Weed control can be problematic around melon plants. While melons can be mulched with straw or chopped leaves, early season crops can also be sown around melons to maximize garden space and cover large swaths of bare soil. Melon plants can also be sown with white clover for a living mulch.

Melons grow sweeter and more readily in warm conditions. If the weather is too cool, the final product might taste much less sweet than its grocery store counter-part. Row covers can create comfortable warm conditions in cooler climates. As a bonus, they can help to keep out squash vine borers or cucumber beetles. Make sure to remove the row covers once the vines begin to flower to allow for pollination. The first flowers are males, so don't panic if you miss them. It's actually helpful if the covers are left on the beds for a week or so. If you're attempting to grow melons in a cooler climate, look for varieties that have shorter timetables from seed to harvest, and keep in mind that the same melons will take longer in cooler environments.

Melons easily cross-pollinate with each other, and sometimes, it can weaken their sweet flavor. If planting two or more variations, try to separate as much as possible.

To Harvest:

With cantaloupe, the skin will turn harder, and ridges will form on the skin. The melon will slip off the vine with a light touch and it will smell much more fragrant. With other varieties of muskmelons, the melon exterior will gradually turn color and look more like the variety pictured on your original seed packet. For watermelons, the task is a bit more challenging. Watermelons will only ripen on the vine, so be careful to remove it from the vine only after you're sure it's ready. To determine its readiness, let your eyes travel up the vine from the fruit until you find a little tendril. Once that tendril turns brown, the fruit is ready to pick.

Foes:

Squash bine borers and squash bugs can attack melon plants. See page 213 for more details.

Potatoes and melons do not mix well and should not be interplanted.

SEED POSSIBILITIES:

For cantaloupes/muskmelons:

Amish Muskmelons (H)—long oval shaped fruits that reach 9 inches in length and weigh 4-7 lbs.; sweet tasting and smelling flesh; prolific vines that produce in a multitude of conditions—*80-90 days*

Eden's Gem/Rocky Ford (H)—short season variety for northern climates, sweet/and slightly spicy flavor; tiny 1-3 lb. melons; green interior, and ribbed exterior—*80-90 days*

Delicious 51 Muskmelon (OP)—short season variety; high yielding vines with small 3-4 lb. melons; orange flesh with sweet scent; demonstrates resistance to powdery mildew—*75-85 days*

Hale's Best Muskmelon (H)—long standing in popularity; generates 5 lb. melons with thick, juicy flesh; shows drought resistance and resistance to powdery mildew—*86 days*

Minnesota Midget (H)—short 3-4 foot vines make this variety perfect for the kitchen gardener; fruits measure 4 inches; pleasant cantaloupe flavor; orangey yellow flesh; also good choice for northern gardeners with short growing seasons—*70 days*

For watermelons:

Blacktail Mountain (OP)—grows well in many climates; produces sprawling vines up to 10 feet and 6-12 lb. melons; richly green rinds and juicy bright orange flesh; if picked shortly before ripened it will keep for up to 2 months in cold storage—*65-75 days*

Crimson Sweet (OP)—classically shaped melon with alternating green stripes; melons weigh between 15 and 25 lbs.; for larger gardens because the vines will sprawl; produces most reliably in the southeastern part of the U.S.; very few seeds; resistant to fusarium wilt—*85-95 days*

Sugar Baby (OP)—short season variety for climates with a limited growing season; a perfect variety for those with small kitchen gardens; generates round 6-12 lb. melons; plants withstand drought well—*65-75 days*

Onions—*Allium cepa*

Ideal P.H.—6.0-7.5
Feed—light
Light requirements—full sun
Family—allium

Friends:

Vegetables: celery, beets, strawberries, carrots, cabbage family crops, potatoes, pumpkins, radishes, squash, Swiss chard, and lettuce
Flowers and Herbs: savory, chamomile

To Grow:

Onions can be grown from set or from seed. Sets are tiny bulbs that were grown from seed the previous year. Sets are easier to grow because they can be planted directly in the garden. Generally, sets are planted about two weeks before the last frost.

Sets will grow vigorously when first planted, but they will ultimately produce smaller bulbs. They're better for early

FOR COMPANION PLANTING

Onions are one of the best companion plants in the garden. Their smell offers protection against pests, and their compact size allows them to be interplanted wherever there is a bit of room.

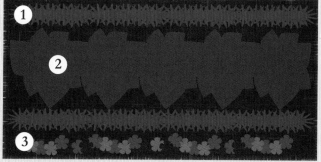

1 - Onions   3 - Nasturtiums
2 - Potatoes

Instead of interplanting potatoes with beans, try interplanting onions with potatoes. It is believed by companion gardeners that the presence of onions will deter the Colorado potato beetle. Make sure to include beans or onions, but not beans and onions.

See page 144 and 149 for other companion planting suggestions.

scallions and can supplement in spring until larger bulbs produce.

If you'd like to produce well-sized onions, consider starting onions from seed. You'll have more options available, and you can choose new varieties each year until you find the variety that grows happiest in your soil. Onion seeds only last one year, so be careful not to be overzealous in your ordering.

In cooler climates, seeds need to be started indoors at least 8 to 10 weeks before the last frost. Onion seeds are planted differently than most seeds starts. Instead of planting the seeds in individual plots, find a plastic bin that measures about 3 inches tall. We take the bottom portion of a seed tray and fill it with potting soil. Sprinkle the onion seeds over top of the soil, and then add an additional 1/2 inch of soil over the top. In the south, seeds can be sown in fall outdoors for a harvest in the spring.

After a few weeks, the onion seeds will have sprouted, and the tray will take on the appearance of freshly sown grass seed. When the seedlings reach 3 inches tall, take some scissors, and chop off the tops of the seedlings. This step will stimulate root production.

When the seedlings are ready for transplant (3 to 4 weeks before the last frost), either create a trough 1½ inches deep, or use a dibble to create holes at that depth. The onion seedlings should be pulled gently from the potting soil and separated at the roots. Each onion seedling will be transplanted with its roots bare. Depending on the onion type, most onion seedlings should be planted 3 to 6 inches apart.

Onions have shallow roots and fare poorly if surrounded by any weeds. Large plantings of onions should be mulched with grass clippings before any weed seeds germinate. When smaller groupings of onions are planted with other garden crops, it makes weed suppression easier. If you do find yourself pulling weeds from onion beds, be careful not to disturb the onion roots. Any disruption will reduce the bulb's ultimate size. It is much better to mulch than to have to pull weeds midway through the growing season.

Onions are not heavy feeders but will benefit from a spray of fish emulsion when they begin to develop bulbs.

To Harvest:

Your onions will let you know when they're finished growing. Their tops will flop over and gradually dry and turn yellow.

Some onions are better for immediate consumption, and others will keep quite well in storage over winter. In most cases, sweet onions are better for fresh eating. When purchasing seeds, seed companies will indicate an onion variety's storage capabilities.

Once the onions have flopped, lay them in the sun to let them cure. When the onions are completely dried, brush the dust from the outside of the bulbs. Be careful not to disturb the exterior onion skin. They can be braided or stored in mesh bags.

Foes:

Onion fly/maggot—The adult onion fly will lay its eggs in close vicinity to onion seedlings. The larvae, and later maggots that develop, will attack the seedlings and the developing bulbs. The damage they create will be very noticeable, even though the maggots themselves only measure about 1/3 of an inch. Make sure to remove infected onions, and do not add them to the compost pile. Companion planting the onions will limit the extent of the damage by isolating the maggots to one area. Crop rotation will discourage maggots the following year.

Members of the allium family pair poorly with any member of the legume family. Make sure to keep onion plantings away from peas or beans in the garden beds.

SEED POSSIBILITIES:

When ordering onion seeds, you will notice that they are labeled either short day, long day, or intermediate. The "short day" label indicates that bulbs will begin to form once the sun is shining 10 to 12 hours. Long day onions won't form bulbs until the days are 14 to 16 hours. Generally speaking, southern farmers below the 35th parallel should grow short day onions, and those above the 35th parallel should grow long day onions. Intermediate onions are more relaxed in their requirements and will grow in most locations. Short day onions generally produce sweeter bulbs, and long day onions stay fresh longer in storage.

For fresh eating:

Ailsa Craig (H)—long day; large white/yellow bulbs, have been known to grow up to five pounds—*95 days*

Gladstone Onion (OP)—intermediate, medium-sized white bulbs; sweet flavor; can grow to a very large size—*110 days*

Walla Walla (OP)—intermediate; Spanish sweet onion; mild, juicy sweet flavor—*105 days*

For storage:

Copra (F1)—intermediate, yellow onion; excellent keeper; is known to store up to 9 to 12 months

Ruby Ring (F1)—long day; offers excellent long-term storage for a red onion—*110-125 days*

Stuttgarter (OP)—yellow onion; known for its ability to keep in storage; sharp pungent flavor—*100-125 days*

Parsnips—*Pastinaca sativa*

Ideal P.H.—6.0-7.0
Feed—heavy
Light requirements—full sun to light shade
Family—carrot

Friends:

Vegetables: bush beans, corn, garlic, melons, onions, peas, peppers, potatoes, radishes, and squash
Herbs and Flowers: love-in-a-mist and marigolds

FOR COMPANION PLANTING

Seed parsnips next to garlic early in the spring. Leave enough space between the two plants so that the roots of the parsnips are not disturbed when the garlic is pulled. Add some peppers in the surrounding space and tuck some love-in-a-mist in around the corners. When the garlic is pulled from the bed in mid-summer, plant some beets, turnips, or salad greens in the freed space.

1 - Garlic   3 - Love-in-a-Mist
2 - Parsnips 4 - Peppers

To Grow:

Parsnips can be planted in early spring, as soon as the ground thaws and the soil can be worked, and while the soil is still cool. The seeds should be sown thickly 1/2 of an inch deep in loose sandy soil, covered with a layer of burlap and kept moist until they germinate. Parsnips can grow to over a foot in length, so they favor the loose soil

> Parsnips seeds do not hold their viability for more than a year. If you purchase a packet of seeds, either plant them all or split them with a gardening friend.

of a raised bed. Like carrots, germination is slow with parsnip seeds, so be patient.

Thin your parsnips with scissors as they grow. Each should ultimately be spaced

4 inches apart (like carrots, they can be thinned by planting radishes in the same row). Parsnips should be mulched heavily to keep the soil moisture level even.

To Harvest:

Parsnips can be harvested on an as needed basis once they have grown more than 120-130 days, and after a hard frost. They can also be covered with mulch, and harvested through the winter, and into the spring. I like to save some of mine for late March or early April. They're one of the few fresh items available at the end of winter.

Foes:

Parsnips don't face many enemies in the garden. They can be attacked by carrot rust flies, but this can be avoided through crop rotation.

Parsnips do not like to be planted with other members of the carrot family, including carrots, celery, or caraway.

SEED POSSIBILITIES:

Harris Model (OP)—long 12" roots; smooth and straight; sweet and nutty in flavor; a standard variety that has been grown for generations—*120 days*

Lancer (OP)—nice sweet flavor; reliable in production—*120 days*

Peas—*Pisum sativum*

Ideal P.H.—6.0-7.0
Feed—soil builder
Light requirements—full
Family—legume

Friends:

Vegetables and Fruits: beans, salad greens, carrots, corn, cucumbers, radishes, and turnips
Flowers and Herbs: Peas have few pests, so the flowers and herbs planted nearby should be based on the plant companions.

To Grow:

Pea seeds will germinate in cool early spring weather, as soon as the soil can be worked. In most climates, gardeners are able to grow both a spring and fall crop. I've found it helpful to inoculate all of my legume seeds, and peas also benefit from inoculation. (See page 135). Peas are sensitive to root disturbance, so make sure to plant them in a weed-free area, and mulch to prevent weeds from germinating. As peas are soil builders, they rarely need any fertilizer during the growing season.

The seeds should be planted at a depth of 1 inch deep and spaced 1 to 2 inches apart. Little seedlings will shoot straight up from the earth within two weeks.

Pay careful attention to the final height of your pea plants when planting the seeds. Some peas will need only a small 2-3 feet trellis, while others, like the *Tall Telephone Garden Peas*, or *Champion of England*, require a trellis of at least 6 feet. This past year, I had mine growing on a trellis that stretched over a pathway between two beds. The peas' placement in the garden can be especially beneficial, as a trellis of peas can offer shade to spinach, lettuce, and other cool weather crops. Shorter peas can be trellised with a quick scattering of twigs.

> The kitchen gardener might find that they don't have the space to grow peas in any great quantity. If the shelled peas you've grown previously could fit in the palm of your hand, try growing snap peas, or grow them just for their flowers. *Dwarf Gray Sugar* peas have glorious purple blooms. *Tom Thumb* peas can be grown in a container.

To Harvest:

Harvesting peas can be tricky if you haven't grown them before. Watch the pods carefully as they grow. The peapods will grow round before the peas actually reach their full size. I usually feel the peapods to make sure the peas have grown plump within. Peas can also be dried on the vine for winter storage.

Harvest your peas every other day to stimulate further production on the vines. Peapods can also be harvested earlier if you'd prefer to utilize the full pod. Certain varieties are preferable for snow or snap peas.

Once you've finished harvesting the vines, cut them at the root to remove the vine. The nutrient rich roots can be tilled back into the soil.

FOR COMPANION PLANTING

1. Shorter pea varieties, like *Dwarf Grey Sugar*, can be grown alongside tomato cages in early spring. The peas will begin growing before the tomatoes have even been transplanted. The tomato seedling can be transplanted within the cages once the soil temperature has reached 60 degrees. The pea vines will also act as a barrier against harsh wind for the tomato seedlings.

   Since tomatoes are heavy feeders, they will likely benefit from the extra nitrogen provided by the peas. If you know your soil is already rich with nitrogen, this combination should be avoided, as a surplus of nitrogen can cause tomatoes to produce only foliage and not fruit.

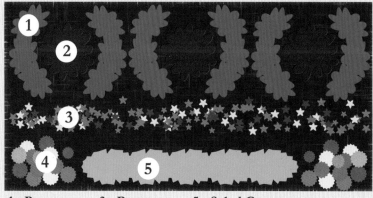

1 - Peas	3 - Borage	5 - Salad Greens
2 - Tomatoes	4 - Marigolds	

2. Peas could also be interplanted with salad greens, carrots, radishes, or turnips. If planted on a shade-providing trellis, the peas grow alongside the greens in early spring, and then are swapped out with beans at the midpoint of summer.

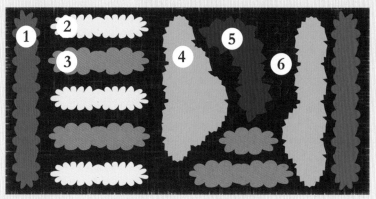

1 - Peas	3 - Carrots	5 - Spinach
2 - Turnips	4 - Salad Greens	6 - Radishes

Foes:

Peas don't have many pests. They are most vulnerable when they first pop out of the soil and can be attacked by slugs during the first few weeks of their growth. If you've seen slugs in your garden previously, place a wooden board on the side of the pea seedlings. The slugs will crawl onto the boards, and the boards can easily be removed from the garden.

Like other legumes, peas do not grow well near alliums. Avoid planting them in close proximity to onions, leeks, garlic, or shallots.

SEED POSSIBILITIES:

Pea seeds are divided into shelling, snap, and snow varieties.

For shelling:

Green Arrow (OP)—plants reach 2½ feet tall; double pods contain 8-11 peas each; sweet flavored; multi-purpose, can be canned, frozen or eaten fresh; disease resistant—*68 days*

Lincoln (OP)—very heat tolerant; produces well in warm climates; generates tender sweet peas; multi-purpose, can be canned, frozen, or eaten fresh—*65-70 days*

Tall Telephone (H)—vines will grow 7-8 feet in height; pods hold 6-8 peas; will produce for several weeks; can be frozen or eaten fresh—*75-85 days*

For snap beans:

Cascadia (OP)—vines grow 3 feet tall; produces stringless plump pods; often touted as an improvement over *Sugar Ann;* trellis for a heavier harvest—*60-70 days*

Amish (H)—long standing heirloom; vines reach 5-6 feet in height; will grow pods for a month and a half if continually picked; sweet flavored—*60-70 days*

For snow peas:

Dwarf Grey Sugar (H)—lovely two toned flowers—lilac and red; great for those with limited space; edible foliage; 2-3 inch pods; vines reach between 2 and 2½ feet; will grow better with trellising—*60 days*

Mammoth Melting Sugar (H)—produces best in cooler climates; delicious 4-5 inch pods; vines grow 5 feet tall—*60 days*

Peppers—*Capsicum annuum*

Ideal P.H.—6.8
Feed—heavy
Light requirements—full sun
Family—nightshade

Friends:

Vegetables and Fruits: carrots, eggplants, onions, parsnips, and tomatoes
Flowers and Herbs: catnip, chives, leeks, marigolds, nasturtiums, and parsley

To Grow:

Peppers are a heat-loving crop. If growing from seed, the seeds need to be started at least a month and a half before your local frost date. The seedlings should only be transferred outside after the daily low temperatures are above 55 degrees. When planting, the seedlings should be transplanted at least a foot apart from each other.

Some tall varieties benefit from staking midway through the season. To stake a pepper plant, cut four or five twigs and place them in the soil around the plant. The extra support will help to keep the plant upright.

Peppers benefit from a light dose of magnesium to help them generate fruit. Place a teaspoon's worth beneath the transplants at the time of planting. In case you forget, you can also make a solution of Epsom salt and water, and spray the solution on the blossoms as they appear during the growing season to make sure the fruit sets.

Pepper plants should be mulched to ensure an adequate moisture level during the growing season. Try mulching with grass clippings or straw.

To Harvest:

When sweet peppers first appear on the plants, they will be green in color. If you leave them on the plant for a few weeks, they will gradually turn from green to yellow, orange, red, or purple. Make sure to remove all the peppers before frost.

Hot peppers can be harvested on a more regular basis from the plants.

Be extremely careful when chopping hot peppers. Wear rubber gloves, even when cleaning the cutting board. During my first experience with hot peppers, I was meticulous with the actual chopping but washed the cutting board with my bare hands. I had hot pepper juice under my nails for days. Ouch!

FOR COMPANION PLANTING

1. Strong smelling herbs and flowers protect peppers from pests. One study indicated that marigolds reduced the number of aphids on pepper plants. Companion gardeners have also noticed that other aromatic herbs, like catnip or nasturtiums, seem to have a similar protective quality. The interplanting will also protect peppers from sunscald. Sunscald develops when peppers are exposed to direct sunlight. See page 164 for a bed interplanted with marigolds, basil, spinach, and eggplants.

| 1 - Basil | 3 - Leeks | 5 - Chives |
| 2 - Marigolds | 4 - Pepper | |

2. Another study indicated that chives and leeks had a similar repellent effect on aphids.

Foes:

Peppers, particularly hot peppers, don't suffer from many attacks by pests. Their distinct flavor provides them with a natural defense. They're often the happiest plants in our garden. Peppers can suffer from attacks by aphids; however, the severity of the attack is dramatically weakened when peppers are companion planted.

In warmer climates, pepper plants can suffer from root knot nematodes. The nematodes live below the soil and are only visible through a microscope. Most likely, you would only see the symptoms of their presence. Plants infected with root knot nematodes will wilt, and their production will be stunted. When the plants are pulled from the garden beds, the roots will exhibit tumorlike growths. If you notice any evidence of root knot nematodes in a garden bed, plant marigolds as a cover crop, and till them into the soil at the end of the season.

Like other nightshade family plants, peppers should not be planted with fennel, potatoes, or kohlrabi.

SEED POSSIBILITIES:

Ace (F1)—prolific performer in cool climates; generates red sweet bell peppers within a short time period—*70 days*

Bulgarian Carrot (OP)—small peppers that look like tiny carrots; crunchy yellow/orange fruits that measure 3½" long; unique hot and fruity taste—*70-80 days*

California Wonder Bell (H)—excellent red bell peppers; plants reach 24-30" while free standing; gorgeous fruit in a variety of climates—*75 days*

Charleston Belle Pepper—a sweet tasting pepper that has also shown resistance to nematodes, compact plants of 18"—*67 days*

Corno di Toro (H)—giant 8-10" sweet peppers; large tall plants that might require some support; fantastic flavor—*75 days*

Maya Red Habanero (OP)—pretty "lantern shaped" peppers that can taste fantastic green or red, hot flavor; a short season variety; productive plants—*90 days (for red peppers)*

Ring of Fire Cayenne (OP)—bright red 4" hot peppers; dependable production; early season ripened, and thin skin for drying—*60 days*

Potatoes—*Solanum tuberosum*

Ideal P.H.—4.8-6.0
Feed—light
Light requirements—full
Family—nightshade

Friends:

Vegetables: beans, cabbage, corn, eggplants, horseradish, peas, and brassica family crops
Herbs and Flowers: savory, basil, parsley, coriander, and marigolds

To Grow:

Potatoes can be planted in spring, around three weeks before the last frost. The soil temperature should be about 60 degrees.

FOR COMPANION PLANTING

1. Try interplanting potatoes with bush beans. Gardeners have noted a mutually beneficial effect. The beans' scent confuses potato beetles, and the potatoes confuse Mexican bean beetles. As potato beetles search out potato plants by smell, strongly

1 - Beans   3 - Potatoes
2 - Nasturtiums   4 - Celery

odorous flowers and herbs can mask the potato plant. Scientific studies noted that nasturtiums, catnip, and coriander all led to a reduction in potato beetles.
2. As an alternative, try adding seed potatoes to a bed of salad greens, radishes, and herbs. The salad greens and radishes will act as short season companions to the potatoes, and they will be gone long before the potato tubers are dug.

1 - Radishes   3 - Potatoes   5 - Basil
2 - Marigolds   4 - Salad Greens   6 - Parsley

3. See page 181 for an example of potatoes intercropped with onions.

If you've had particular problems with the Colorado potato beetle, they can be planted later in the summer to lessen the likelihood of damage. Those in warmer climates can generally produce two harvests—one in spring, and one in fall.

If you're short on space, potatoes easily grow in containers also. Stick a few purple potatoes in pots on the patio, and let the pretty purple flowers decorate the edges of your outdoor living space.

> It is best to purchase your seed potatoes from a local nursery or online. Potatoes sold in the grocery store have been sprayed with a chemical to prevent sprouting.

Potatoes are cultivated on a yearly basis through the use of "seed" potatoes. Seed potatoes are simply potatoes that have been held back from the previous year's stock. When potatoes are removed from cold storage and brought into warmer air, they will start to grow "eyes." This process is called "chitting." Before your seed potatoes are placed in the ground, they need to show some sprouts from their eyes.

Some gardeners prefer to slice their seed potatoes into smaller pieces with an eye on each piece. In that case, the potatoes are left on a tray for several days to form a layer of skin over the raw edge. I skip this extra step, and I just plant my potatoes whole. It probably reduces the output and size of my potatoes somewhat, but I prefer the convenience.

Potatoes should be planted in a trench in the ground that has been dug just under a foot deep. Each seed potato should be separated about a foot apart; larger whole potatoes should be given a bit more room. Once the potatoes are laid in the trench, cover them with a layer of soil. Leave some of the soil to cover the potatoes once they have poked through the first layer. If your soil is heavy, try using straw for the first layer instead. If you decided not to plant your potatoes in a trench, the soil should be hilled around the potatoes once the plants reach about 8 to 10 inches tall.

To Harvest:

Potatoes hold a magical quality. They're quite fun to grow with children. They won't be picked early by overeager hands, and as each potato is uncovered

at harvest, they generate little squeals of delight. Fortunately, one does not need children to experience this joy.

You can harvest a few tiny "new" potatoes once your plants have flowered for a week or so. Feel around the potato plants with your hands and pick one or two from the plant. If you decided to grow your potatoes in straw, this process is even easier. Although it may feel like you're robbing the plant while it's still in progress, the remaining potatoes will grow larger and stronger.

You'll know the rest of your potatoes are ready to harvest once the plants have begun to yellow and wither away. Don't

leave the potatoes in the ground for too long after the plant has died, or the potatoes will begin to rot.

Foes:

Colorado Potato Beetle—The Colorado potato beetle is the most ambitious foe of the potato plant. Colorado potato beetles have hard shells with well-defined black and yellow stripes. They measure just under half of an inch long. The beetles and their larvae will quickly strip the plants of their leaves.

A healthy layer of mulch can discourage the beetles. Straw or rotted leaf mulch will provide a habitat for beneficial insects. It will also impede the beetles' approach.

Potatoes have numerous foes. Pumpkins, tomatoes, squash, sunflowers, and cucumbers can all make potatoes more susceptible to blight. Potatoes are also known to stunt the growth of several garden plants, including tomatoes. The presence of garlic actually led to an increase in potato beetles.

SEED POSSIBILITIES:

Seed potatoes will be labeled as early, mid-, or late season potatoes. If you'd prefer to eat your potatoes during the summer, an early or mid-season variety is best. If you'd like to try cold storing your potatoes, try a late season variety instead.

Early Season:

Irish Cobbler (H)—light brown skin and white flesh; medium-sized tubers; consistent and reliable

Peanut (H)—fingerling potatoes with golden skin and yellow flesh; high yields and long-term storage

Purple Viking (H)—large purple skinned potatoes with white flesh; superior flavor; compact plants that can be grown in containers; demonstrated resistance to scab

Mid-Season:

Purple Majesty (H)—unique tubers with purple skin and flesh, should be eaten fresh

Russian Banana (H)—easy and prolific fingerling potatoes with yellow skin and white flesh, exceptional taste, compact plants with high yields

Late Season:

Elba—large tubers with tan skin and white flesh; noted for their resistance to scab and blight; stores well

German Butterball (H)—golden yellow skin and yellow flesh; prolific plants; fantastic flavor; great for long-term storage

Kennebec (H)—large potatoes with yellow skin and white flesh; dependable; disease resistant plants; bear heavy yields; good storage

Radishes—*Raphanus sativus*

Ideal P.H.—5.8-6.8
Feed—light
Light requirements—full sun and partial shade
Family—brassica

If some radishes are left to flower, the pretty pink blooms will attract beneficials, and then the plants will eventually grow pods. The pods are also edible. Try *Rat's Tail* or *Madras Podding* for the best tasting pods.

Friends:

Vegetables: radishes have many friends, including lettuce, carrots, onions, and crops in the brassica, cucurbit, and legume families
Flowers and Herbs: nasturtiums and marigolds

FOR COMPANION PLANTING
Radishes are commonly utilized as a trap crop for flea beetles. I've included them in quite a few garden bed designs. Check out pages 134, 162, 179 and 188.

To Grow:

If you're looking to plant an easy crop in your starter garden that will grow quickly and thrill your children, start with radishes.

Plant radish seeds outdoors in early spring, and plant several small successions over the course of a month. Seeds should be spaced 1 to 2 inches apart and 1/2 of an inch deep. Tiny radish seedlings will sprout within days. Radishes grow best in the spring and fall, when temperatures are cooler. They aren't specific about soil requirements, but they do need an even level of moisture and relatively loose soil. Radishes that spend too much time in dry soil will taste woody and bitter.

In a companion planted garden, radishes are usually placed around other companion crops. As long as they're tucked away under companions, don't be too concerned about mulching.

To Harvest:

Harvest radishes while they're still small. They will keep growing (I've found hidden radishes that reached the size of a russet potato), but the taste suffers.

Foes:

Radishes are known more for their reputed repelling capabilities and their utilization as a trap crop. Still, radishes themselves can be attacked by common brassica family foes, like cabbage maggots. Flea beetles will bite radish leaves, but the damage is much reduced if the radishes are companion planted.

SEED POSSIBILITIES:

Radish seeds are divided into categories depending upon how many hours of daylight they take to produce a bulb. I'm more partial to spring and fall varieties because there's so much else to harvest from the garden during the summer.

Spring radishes:

Cherry Belle (H)—easily productive; 1" radishes with pink skin and white flesh— *22 days*

Early Scarlet Globe (H)—cute 1" radishes with bright pinkish red skin and white crisp interior; grows well in sandy soil—*20-28 days*

French Breakfast (H)—these radishes grow better in cooler weather; generate a longer taproot than most (2-3") in a short time span; deep scarlet skin towards the top—*25-30 days*

Helios (H)—sunny colored pale yellow skin with white flesh; more sweet and mild than many radishes—*30-35 days*

Fall/Winter radishes:

Miyashige (H)—a Japanese daikon white radish that grows 16-18" into the ground; sow in midsummer for a fall harvest, roots keep in storage up to 9 months—*50 days*

China Rose (H)—bright pink color; taproot reaches 4-5" with a rounded end; can survive frost—*50-60 days*

Salad Greens

Lettuce—*Lactuca sativa*

Ideal P.H.—6.0-6.7
Feed—light to moderate
Light requirements—full sun to partial shade
Family—aster (lettuce)

Friends:

Vegetables and Fruit: beets, carrots, garlic, onions, parsnips, radishes, and strawberries

Flowers and Herbs: salad greens grow well with many flowers and herbs. Choose companions based on neighboring cultivars.

To Grow:

Salad greens grow best in the cooler temperatures of the spring and fall, when the temperatures are between 55 and 75 degrees. To sow leafy salad green seeds, start your first succession 6 to 8 weeks before your last frost date, and keep sowing every two weeks through spring. Place the seeds on the soil surface, and cover with a sprinkling of soil. Salad greens often germinate unevenly and depending on the variety, greens can take between two days and two weeks to germinate. Heading salad greens should be given more growing space when seeded—between 7 to 10 inches. Keep the soil around your lettuce relatively damp as the lettuce matures. Lettuce has shallow roots, and if the plants dry out, they will turn bitter earlier in the season.

> If this is your first year gardening, I implore you to start with salad greens. They can be grown in containers, they don't suffer from much abuse by pests, they can be clipped over and over, and you can eat them every day!
>
> The term "salad greens" represents a broad category of mustards, arugula, and lettuces. Here I've highlighted those greens I feel work best for those cultivating kitchen gardens. In the seed possibilities section, I suggest alternatives to traditional lettuce. I've noted any variance in growing requirements with the seed description.

FOR COMPANION PLANTING

Nearly every garden bed I've designed contains some room for lettuce or salad greens. Lettuce nestles most sweetly with onions, carrots, garlic, and radishes. See pages 137, 172, 188, 209 and 219 for some inspiration.

To Harvest:

Harvest your leafy greens through thinning, or as soon as they reach a reasonable size for cutting. As a companion gardener, you should have small patches of greens growing throughout the garden. You can start harvesting greens from the garden much earlier than the traditional gardener who has reserved their greens patch to one minuscule spot. I've noticed that my greens tend to grow more quickly if I trim them early and often. Head lettuce can also be harvested early on, but if you wish to be able to grow full heads, leave this lettuce alone for at least a couple of months.

Once the greens send forth stalks and sprout flowers, they are past the season for picking. Greens harvested in weather past 80 degrees will taste bitter and unappetizing. They're really just horrible at this point, so catch the seeds if you can. Otherwise, rip up the plants to make room for something new.

Foes:

The most likely foe of lettuce is the common garden slug—see page 122 for possible remedies.

SEED POSSIBILITIES:

Lettuce—When purchasing lettuce seeds for a smaller garden, I'd highly suggest picking a leaf lettuce variety pack. Most seed companies sell variety packs, and you can choose according to color and taste.

Other Salad Greens:

Arugula (Rocket)—Rocket deserves its name in a garden because it appears to germinate and grow faster than any other edible. It does have a bit of a bitter taste, but it becomes milder when grown in cooler weather. Harvest the leaves while the plant is still in its "baby" stage for the best taste. For zones 6 and higher, arugula can be grown throughout the winter—*21-40 days*

Claytonia (Miner's Lettuce)—Claytonia is a winter hardy green that can be grown overwinter in zones 6 and warmer. A perennial in warmer climates, it can grow somewhat aggressively if allowed to spread. It will thrive in full sun and partial sun—*40-60 days*

Mustard—There are a plethora of mustard greens on the market. Most of them have a spicy kick that grows stronger as the greens grow larger. My favorite is *Tatsoi*, a green that will keep growing in cool weather—*25-45 days*

Squash (includes pumpkins, zucchini, butternut, acorn, yellow and winter squash)

Summer squash—*Cucurbita pepo*
Winter squash and pumpkin—*Cucurbita spp.*
Ideal P.H.—5.5-6.8
Feed—heavy
Light requirements—full sun
Family—cucurbit

Friends:

Vegetables: beans, celeriac, celery, corn, lettuce, spinach, onions, and radishes
Herbs and Flowers: catnip (in pots), clover, dill, fennel, nasturtiums, marigolds, sunflowers, sweet asylum, and yarrow

---

FOR COMPANION PLANTING

1. For squashes with a bush habit, like zucchini or summer squash, place the plants in the center of a bed with some radishes around the top of the mounds. Add lettuce, clover, spinach, or sweet alyssum in the bare space early in the season. By midsummer, the squash will take over the area available. Squash varieties do cross-pollinate within a species, so don't include zucchini and summer squash in the same bed.

1 - Dill   3 - Radishes   5 - Spinach
2 - Summer Squash 4 - Sweet Aslyum 6 - Salad Greens

2. To companion plant vining squashes, I highly suggest a trellis. Pick crops to surround the squash at the base that will attract predatory insects and pollinators. It is often recommended to separate varieties within a species by 1/8 of a mile if you plan on saving the seed. In the past, I've set up a trellis for winter squash on either end of the garden, and I haven't noticed any cross-pollination within the season.

To Grow:

Most gardeners start their squash and pumpkin seeds outside, though transplants can be utilized to extend the growing season (and to beat a pest infestation or powdery mildew).

Plant seeds at a depth of 1 inch in raised mounds of soil that have been enriched with some compost or leaf mold. For bush squash, give each hill 1½ feet of space all the way around. If you plan to grow vining squash plants, you will need a larger bed to keep the squash contained. A trellis can be helpful for those with smaller gardens. Trellises can also discourage the spread of powdery mildew by allowing more airflow between the vines.

Once the seedlings appear, leave only the two strongest in each hill, and cut the stragglers. Mulch around the plants to deter weed growth. Because the plants are spaced at a great width initially, weeds can overtake a bed before the vines cover the ground. During the growing season, spray them with fish emulsion or aerated compost tea each month. The aerated compost tea can slow the development of powdery mildew.

> If your vines are only meant for a designated area in your garden, pinch the tips of the vines once they start to creep over the sides. The plants will then turn their energy towards fruit production.

You can see the difference between male squash blossoms and female squash blossoms here. Female blossoms are much larger, and male blossoms extend upward more.

A squash bug nymph crawling on a pumpkin

To Harvest:

Harvest zucchini and summer squash once they reach 7 or 8 inches in length. Sometimes zucchini hide among the vines and aren't found until they've grown to the size of a toddler's wiffle bat. In that case, I cut them lengthwise and throw them to the chickens. I've had late season zucchini last in cold storage until January, so don't feel pressured to eat them all at once.

Pumpkins, butternut, and winter squash are ready to harvest when the stem of the fruit turns color, hardens, and dries. Trim the fruit from the vines with a sharp knife, and transfer the squash to a warm and shady location for curing.

Foes:

The Squash Bug—The most ardent foe of any squash plant is undoubtedly the squash bug. Adult squash bugs are 1/2 or 3/4 inches in length, and their backs are a muted brownish gray. They will attack your squash plants by sucking any nutrients from the leaves, and the leaves will gradually wither and die. Of all the bugs hated by organic gardeners, squash bugs seem to generate the most vitriol.

Although it may seem cliché, the best defense against squash bugs is prevention. As your squash plants grow, continually check the undersides of the leaves near the primary vein. Squash bugs lay tiny brownish orange eggs in little clusters. The eggs can be squished between your forefinger and thumb, and they will never have a chance to hatch. Although this process is tedious and cumbersome, it does work.

If you've had an entire squash plant bed demolished by squash bugs, try row covers the next season. Only uncover the plants about a week after the first flower blooms, so pollination can occur. Also, consider planting a few of your squash plants among your front flowerbeds. The squash will be well hidden among the flowers and herbs, and they will be less susceptible to a squash bug infestation. Squash bugs are also a favorite food of parasitic wasps. Including your squash plants directly in a perennial bed that is full of flowers and herbs will attract the wasps, and the squash bugs will provide them with a steady diet of food.

Finally, there are some squash varieties that are resistant to squash bugs—try *Early Summer Crookneck, Improved Green Hubbard, Butternut,* or *Royal Acorn.*

The Squash Vine Borer—Squash vine borers are also known to cause headaches for many gardeners. The larvae—1 inch, off white, wormlike insects—drill tunnels into the stems of squash plants. The plants wilt, and they often die. Predatory insects don't really attack the larvae because the borers are often hidden inside the plant.

Organic gardeners have devised many methods to prevent squash vine borers from killing their squash plants. The borers typically enter the plant around the base of the main vines, so gardeners will wrap the base with aluminum foil to prevent entry. Hubbard squashes are often grown as a trap crop. The adult moths are also attracted to yellow bowls filled with water and will drown once they enter.

If your squash plants have previously withered from damage caused by squash vine borers, floating row covers are your best option to prevent another infestation. If you're only growing a couple plants on a trellis, protect the vines with aluminum instead.

The larvae spend the winter among previously diseased plants, so any infected vines should be destroyed and not composted.

Squash should not be planted among potato plants. It's been observed that the potato plant can stunt the growth of squash.

SEED POSSIBILITIES:

Summer Squash:

Dark Star (OP)—dark green fruits with a mellow flavor; deep roots make this variety drought tolerant; tolerant of cooler weather; long growth season—*50 days*

Golden Zucchini Squash (OP)—compact bush plant (3-4') perfect for small spaces; mild flavored yellow squash—*55 days*

Raven (F1)—dark green fruits, pale white flesh with a mild taste, bush plant—2' tall and 3' wide, heavy yield in small spaces—*45 days*

Scallop Yellow Squash (H)—bush plant perfect for small gardens; grows "patty pan" type squash with a creamy texture and flavoring; grows easily and produces for a long season—*50 days*

Zephyr (F1)—unique yellow fruits with a pale green tip, very high yield, mild and delicious flavor—*54 days*

Winter Squash:

Baby Blue Hubbard (OP)—gorgeous pale gray/blue skin and sweet flesh; these vines are more compact than the standard Hubbard squash; can be sacrificed as "trap" crop for squash vine borers or cucumber beetles—*95 days*

Baby Pan Pumpkin (OP)—popular variety for flavor; fruits weigh 3-4 lbs.; skin is dark orange and lovely for fall decorations; yields 4-5 fruits per plant; perfect for the kitchen gardener—*100 days*

Honey Bear Acorn (F1)—compact bush plant; yields 4" acorn fruits that weigh around 1 lb.; flesh is yellow, sweet, and mild; plants have demonstrated powdery mildew resistance—*85-100 days*

New England Pumpkin (OP)—4-8 lb. pumpkins perfect for pies; a long-standing favorite among gardeners—*100 days*

Waltham Butternut (OP)—yield pale orange uniform fruits with sweet flesh; keep up to 9 months in storage—*105 days*

Spinach—*Spinacia oleracea*

Ideal P.H.—6.5-7.2
Feed—moderate
Light requirements—full sun to partial shade
Family—spinach

Friends:

Vegetables and Fruits: Brussels sprouts, cabbage, celery, eggplants, onions, peas, peppers, and strawberries
Flowers and Herbs: borage, cosmos, dill, and yarrow

FOR COMPANION PLANTING

Spinach isn't picky and will happily live among many vegetables in your garden. Try planting it among strawberries and borage in the fall to hold back weeds. It can also be planted in the shade of beans, peas, brassicas or many other edibles. See pages 134, 162, 164 and 188 for examples.

To Grow:

Spinach is a cool weather crop. It's one of the earliest annuals I direct seed in our outdoor garden in the spring, and one of the last annuals I seed in the fall. As soon as the soil can be worked, spinach seeds can be planted in the ground. It grows best in temperatures below 75 degrees, so in our area it works best as a spring and fall crop. If you live in a warmer climate, spinach should be saved for the winter months.

It's also possible to grow spinach in the shade of taller vegetation during the warmer months. However, if a heat wave (85 degrees or more) lingers for more than one or two days, the spinach crop will likely turn bitter and unappetizing, and soon it will bolt and flower.

Spinach seeds should be planted 1/2 of an inch deep. Depending on the configuration of your garden beds, it can be planted as an edging, and a spacer, or in its own bed surrounded by low growing flowers.

To Harvest:

Spinach will "cut and come again" to a limited extent. It tastes sweetest when it's small, so don't be afraid to snip a few leaves while they are still an inch or less in width. Continually trimming the leaves will actually make the plant produce faster.

Foes:

Spinach Leafminers—Spinach leafminers most commonly appear on spinach and Swiss chard. They lay white eggs on the undersides of leaves and once the larvae hatch, they will burrow through the leaves and leave telltale white meandering lines. Crush the eggs with your fingers before they hatch, or snip the infected leaves. Parasitic wasps often eat leafminers so make sure some attractive flowers are planted at a close range.

SEED POSSIBILITIES:

Buy several kinds of spinach seeds to see which ones best suit your soil. Also, make sure to factor the season into your seed selection. Some spinach varieties are more heat tolerant, and others grow better in cool conditions.

Giant Winter Spinach (H)—cool weather variety recommended for overwintering; produces a heavy yield of dark green leaves—*45 days*

New Zealand (H)—slight variant of spinach, actually thrives in warmer weather and will grow as a perennial in warm climates; tolerates heat and drought; tastes great cooked—*50-60 days*

Orach/Mountain Spinach—an alternative to spinach that is less likely to bolt in warm weather; leaves stay sweeter in warm weather; leaves are often red and purple and some varieties can reach 4-6'—*28-45 days*

Red Malabar—not actually spinach—this variety has a hint of Swiss chard taste; sprouts dark green leaves and red vines and will regrow rapidly if the vines are cut; trellis for best growth; a personal favorite—*60-70 days*

Renegade (F1)—this hybrid resists bolting remarkably well, produces round dark green leaves, grows in a variety of climates and soil—*42 days*

Tyee (F1)—straight, upright leaves unlikely to bolt; mildew resistant—*45 days*

Winter Bloomsdale (OP)—this variety is perfect for colder climates and overwintering; dark green leaves; slow growth—*47 days*

Sweet Potatoes—*Ipomoea batatas*

Ideal P.H.—5.5-6.5
Feed—light
Light requirements—full sun
Family—convolvulaceae (morning glory)

Friends:

Sweet potato plants send out long runners that will ramble and spread all around and over the length of the garden bed. Because of their sprawling nature, it's unlikely that they can be interplanted with other vegetables within the same plot. I prefer to locate some of my more aromatic potted herbs at a close distance.

To Grow:

Sweet potatoes are grown through "slips," or small potato vines that will sprout from sweet potato tubers. You can grow your own, but if you'd like to grow a unique heirloom variety, you can order slips online.

Sweet potato slips should be planted single file down a garden bed. The tubers will grow best in slightly sandy soil with a bit of bone meal mixed in at the time of planting. Once a wave of warm weather arrives, the sweet potato vines will hit a growth spurt and soon cover the bed.

For northern gardens, I've found it extremely helpful to add row covers over my sweet potatoes. Sweet potatoes love heat, and our climate doesn't generate enough consistently. The row covers remain over the vines for most of the summer. I turn them back when the temperature reaches the nineties. As a clone, sweet potatoes do not require any pollination, so the row covers can remain over the vines when they flower.

To Harvest:

Sweet potatoes have a long growing season; most linger in the ground over 100 days. Heed the frost warnings in the fall, and make sure to dig for your tubers before the first frost. If there is a surprise frost, cut the vines straightaway, and harvest the tubers within the day. While some tubers will be easy to locate at the base of the original slip, others will be found at quite a distance away, in relatively random locations.

If the tubers are cured in a warm (80 to 85 degrees) space for at least 5 days, they can be stored for up to twelve months.

> Sweet potato vines are a popular ornamental, but the tubers that grow from them are not especially good to eat. The propagated vines have typically been treated with chemicals, and the tubers don't taste good anyway.

Foes:

The Sweet Potato Weevil—The female weevil will lay eggs in the sweet potatoes, and then seal the hole with her poop. (I've thought of many poop jokes to insert here, but I thought it best to leave it alone.) Once the larvae hatch, they will burrow throughout the tubers, leaving feces laden holes as they munch. The weevils are more prevalent in the hot humid conditions of the southern states, and on commercial farms. If they ever appear in your garden plot, make sure to crop rotate in successive years. Avoid planting sweet potatoes until the infestation subsides.

> The vines of the sweet potato plant are edible. The leaves make good cooking greens, and the flavor is often compared to spinach.

SEED POSSIBILITIES:

If you'd like to grow more than one variety, but only have limited space, purchase a variety pack. *Southern Exposure* offers an orange, white, and purple pack, and *Sandy Hill Preservation* often offers variety packs.

Beauregard—orange tubers; quicker variety for northern climates; vigorous growth—*95 days*
Georgia Jets—earliest to mature in the south; great baking sweet potato; deep pink exterior and orangey flesh—*80-90 days*
Vardaman—bushing variety of sweet potatoes; fantastic flavor; orange skin and flesh; roots are smaller than average—*90 days*

Swiss Chard—*Beta vulgaris (Cicla group)*

Ideal P.H.—6.0-7.0
Feed—light to moderate
Light requirements—full sun or partial shade
Family—spinach

Friends:

Vegetables: bush beans, garlic, leeks, lettuce, peas, onions, and brassica family members

Flowers and Herbs: Most pests don't bother Swiss chard, so instead of planting flowers alongside to protect the Swiss chard, plant Swiss chard wherever you find room.

To Grow:

Seed Swiss chard in the garden about a month before the frost date, and leave about 4-6 inches of space between each plant. I originally started my Swiss chard for the baby leaves, so my seeds were planted much closer, and then I thinned as the plants reached maturity. The more space each plant has, the larger the leaves will grow. Once the seeds sprout, mulch the sprouts with some chopped leaves to suppress weed competition.

FOR COMPANION PLANTING

Swiss chard fits in perfectly with a bed of greens or spinach, leeks, and lettuce. In warmer climates, it can become perennial, so plan accordingly when first adding to the garden. Swiss chard's colorful stems also blend well in more auspiciously landscaped flower beds.

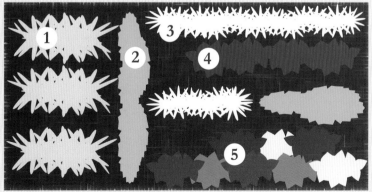

1 - Garlic   3 - Leeks   5 - Swiss Chard
2 - Lettuce   4 - Spinach

To Harvest:

Baby chard leaves can be harvested for use in salads. For full-grown chard, outer leaves should be harvested once the plant stems have grown to half an inch in diameter. Chard is a "cut and come again" green and will produce throughout the summer and into the fall. It can be overwintered in warmer climates and often outlasts zero degree temperatures if protected with a top layer of mulch.

Foes:

Like spinach, Swiss chard is sometimes attacked by leafminers. See page 216 for more details.

SEED POSSIBILITIES:

Fordhook Giant (H)—one of the largest varieties of chard; white stems with striking dark green crinkly leaves; more tolerant of heat than other varieties—*50-60 days*
Rainbow/Five Color Silver Beet (H)—stems turn colors of red, pink, yellow, orange, and white; mild flavor; shoots grow straight for easy picking—*60 days*
Ruby Red/Rhubarb Chard (H)—deeply colored dark red stalks with rich green leaves; fits beautifully in flower beds—*50-60 days*

Tomatoes—*Lycopersicon esculentum*

Ideal P.H.—6.0-7.0
Feed—heavy feeder
Light requirements—full sun
Family—nightshade

Friends:

Vegetables: asparagus, beans, carrots, eggplants, lettuce, peas, peppers, and onions
Flowers and Herbs: borage, cosmos, chives, basil, horehound, marigolds, parsley, and sage

To Grow:

If growing from seed, tomato seedlings should be started indoors about 6 to 8 weeks before the last frost. Plant the seeds at a depth of 1/4 of an inch. Most gardeners transplant the seedlings into a 3 to 4 inch container before they move them to the outdoors.

If you find it necessary to purchase transplants, evaluate the plants carefully. Transplants from garden centers are often held in close quarters, and they can carry diseases that can be easily transferred to your garden. Purchased plants should have healthy dark green leaves, and no signs of wilt.

Tomatoes are a warm weather crop and shouldn't be transplanted to the outdoors until soil temperatures reach about 60 degrees. Tomato transplants are also sensitive to wind, so consider sheltering them with row covers until the spring winds die down. Make sure the transplants are given a home in an area that receives full sun (at least 7 hours).

Don't feel stressed to rush transplanting to the garden once your area has reached its frost date. Although the

The tomato made its first journey to Europe after the conquistadors invaded South America. They were identified as pommes d'amour, and they kept that name, or "love apples," in America until the Revolutionary War.

Somehow, the English missed out on the deliciousness of the tomato and kept them only as ornamentals in the 16th and 17th century. Their opinion didn't change until almost 1800.

transplants may appear smaller than their counterparts at the farmer's market, they catch up during the season. If they're stressed by outdoor weather conditions early on, they'll only languish and stagnate for several weeks before they decide to grow.

Tomatoes love rich soil and some fertilization during the growing season. When setting the transplants in their outdoor home, bury the plants so that only their top leaves are above ground. Some gardeners even flip the plants on their side. Each buried stem will become a supporting root.

Mulching is essential for tomatoes. They are extremely sensitive to any splash back from rain, and the fungal disease will make its way up the plant leaves with each rainfall. Try mulching with chopped leaves, or plant a ground cover of white clover the same day the tomatoes are transplanted to the garden bed.

Gardeners have devised thousands of ways to support tomato plants while they grow. Some prefer to stake their plants, and remove additional suckers, keeping the tomato growth to one or two main vines. If you choose this method, give your plants at least 2 feet of growing space. Others prefer to cage their tomato plants. Still remove suckers, but allow the plants to grow into more of a bushy shape. With this method, the plants should be spaced 3 feet apart.

Either way, many of the tomato vines will need staking, even within the framework of the cage. The amount of vine staking required depends upon the types of tomato plants cultivated. "Determinate" tomatoes grow to more of a bushy shape and will stop growing after they reach about 3 feet tall. With "indeterminate" varieties, it's anyone's guess. Some of mine have reached upwards of 10 feet. Heirloom tomatoes are mostly indeterminate. If you've decided to grow heirlooms in your garden, it is better to stake your plants to allow for their generous growth. I've also seen gardeners hang netting along a row of tomatoes, and guide the vines between the netting as they grow upwards.

I find the removal of suckers during the growing season crucial for two main reasons. First, the increased airflow deters the spread of fungal diseases. Secondly, the removal of superfluous vegetation will force the plants to concentrate their energy towards creating big healthy tomatoes. I have noticed some discussion regarding the necessity of pruning, with the argument that the pruning of suckers actually weakens the plants, hastens its death, and makes it more likely that it will succumb to disease. I'm sure this discussion will continue to be a "hot bed" of discussion in the coming years as wetter conditions seem to be increasingly the norm in our ever-so-warmer climate.

To Harvest:

Tomatoes are easy to spot when ripe, as they'll turn red, or yellow, or some other beautiful color. In warmer climates, remove them from the plant as they begin to blush, and allow them to turn completely on a windowsill indoors. In cooler climates, it may require some patience before the first tomatoes ripen on the vine.

FOR COMPANION PLANTING

1. Tomatoes grow agreeably with peppers, tomatoes, beans, peas, and carrots. In a scientific study, tomatoes demonstrated increased protection against bacterial wilt when they were interplanted with garlic chives. Before interplanting a bed, pay careful attention to the sun's path through the garden. Indeterminate tomatoes will grow to a greater height than most of their companion crops, so make sure they don't shade any of their companions. (See page 134 for an example of tomatoes interplanted with beans.)

1 - Tomatoes   3 - Borage   5 - Lettuce   7 - Chives
2 - Marigolds   4 - Peppers   6 - Basil

2. Indeterminate tomatoes can be trellised along the back side of a garden bed interplanted with carrots and onions.

   Tomatoes also grow nicely with asparagus, but they should only be added to the permanent asparagus beds every 4 years to allow for crop rotation.

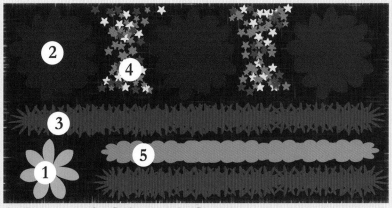

1 - Pepper   3 - Onions   5 - Carrots
2 - Tomato   4 - Borage

While the plants can be protected from frost in the fall with sheets or plastic, it's much easier to just cook the green tomatoes instead. Fried green tomatoes are an obvious choice—also look for green tomato salsa recipes, or try tomato chow-chow.

Whatever you do, never place your tomatoes in the refrigerator. The tomatoes will lose all of their sweet taste.

Foes:

The Tomato Hornworm—The tomato hornworm is probably the most notorious of the garden pests. Although it isn't particularly destructive, it has an appreciative "shock value." Hornworms blend well with tomato plant leaves, but when they are found by the unsuspecting gardener, their bulging eyes, swollen body, and white teeth (actually suction cups) are quite alarming. With a steady diet of tomato leaves, they can grow up to three inches in length. They also create a disgusting, yet satisfying pile of goo, if you happen to squish one with the heel of your shoe.

Hornworms chew large holes in leaves, and if left to devour the leaves without disruption, they will move on to the tomatoes themselves. If you see a slightly shriveled hornworm with little white pills sticking out of its back, the hornworm has been infested with parasitic wasps. Parasitic wasps are beneficial insects, so leave them to suck the life out of the worm. The hornworm will be gone in a few days, and the parasitic wasps will be left to protect your garden.

While studies have shown that tomatoes can protect cabbage from white fly infestations, the cabbage can stunt the growth of the tomato plant. Therefore, unless you have an overflowing bounty of tomatoes, avoid interplanting tomatoes with cabbage.

Tomato plants appreciate consistency during the growing season, and water is an important component. When tomato plants soak in too much water, the tomatoes will crack and split before they ripen. If the tomato plants aren't watered enough, the fruits won't reach full size, or they may develop blossom end rot. Blossom end rot is aptly named, as the end of the tomatoes will shrivel, turn black, and cave in towards the fruit. The rot is often an indication of a calcium deficiency in the soil. I've found that the problem is easily remedied by dampening the roots of any symptomatic plants with some watered down milk.

The most common complaint among gardeners concerning tomatoes relates to the plethora of fungal diseases associated with their demise. To ward off disease from your plants, tomatoes really demand the best soil your garden has to offer. The diseases that manifest on your plants as brown spots, yellow leaves, black dots, or whatever, start their lives as fungus, bacteria, or viruses that habitat in the soil. Those diseases thrive in neglected anaerobic soil.

Tomatoes should also not be planted with fennel, kohlrabi, or potatoes.

Hornworm

SEED POSSIBILITIES:

Ordering tomato seeds can prove a difficult task. There are so many incredible heirloom varieties, and the bright colored photographs and mouthwatering descriptions can make it challenging, if not impossible, to narrow down the list. Consider ordering tomatoes with a friend, and then swapping some of the seeds to increase your heirloom options. Tomato seeds keep for five years.

Also, make sure to consider what you plan to use your tomatoes for once they are harvested. Some tomatoes contain more pulp and are better suited for canning and preserving. Others are more uniquely flavored and are best appreciated in fresh summer salads. Also, some heirloom plants will produce less fruit. For disease resistance, try varieties like *Better Boy, Early Girl, Lemon Boy,* or *Carmello.*

For fresh eating:

Black Krim (H)—beautiful dark red color; smoky wine-like flavor; somewhat disease resistant—*69-90 days*

Brandywine (H)—giant pinkish red fruits; juicy and sweet; wonderful flavor; can be a challenge to grow; susceptible to disease and cracking; vines can reach up to 10 feet—*78 days*

Cherokee Purple (H)—large brownish tomatoes with green shoulders; wine- like sweet flavor; plants provide ample fruit—*80 days*

Green Zebra (OP)—sweet and salty flavor; yellow and green stripes when ripe; produces well in many climates, but is susceptible to blossom end rot—*75-80 days*

For canning or preservation:

Amish Paste (H)—brightly flavored, and perfect for sauces and paste—*85 days*

Roma (OP)—known for its reliability; fleshy tomato; diseases resistant; determinant vines don't require staking—*70-75 days*

San Marzano—Italian paste tomato, great all around tomato for kitchen preservation—*80 days*

For fun:

Dr. Wyche's Yellow (H)—large 1 lb. yellow tomatoes; meaty flesh and mild flavor—*75-85 days*

Indigo Rose (OP)—gorgeous dark red, almost black tomatoes; prolific production; contain antioxidants—*80 days*

Moonglow (H)—midsized orangey yellow tomatoes; reliable productivity—*85 days*

Sun Gold (F1)—sweet orangey yellow cherry tomatoes; vigorous; extended season—*65 days*

Tomatillos—*Physalis philadelphica*

Ideal P.H.—6.0-7.0
Feed—light
Light requirements—full sun
Family—nightshade

Friends:

Vegetables: bush beans, carrots, celery, cucumbers, garlic, onions, and peppers
Flowers and Herbs: basil, calendulas, chives, marigolds, mint, nasturtiums, and parsley

To Grow:

Tomatillos are tomato-shaped fruits with papery husks that burst open as the fruits reach maturity. They're one of the most reliable edibles in our garden. They always produce a heavy crop, and I barely even have to throw them a glance during the growing season.

To grow tomatillos, start seeds when you start your pepper seeds—about 10 weeks

Tomatillos have a friendly cousin called ground cherries. Ground cherries are prolific plants that will often self-sow in your garden year after year, though they are not invasive. They produce marble-sized cherries in a brown paper husk that turn yellow when ripe. They possess a really unique flavor, like a pineapple crossed with a tomato, and we find them absolutely delicious. The fruits often fall to the ground before they're ripe, so you have to root among the leaves to find the fruits. I think they're worth the extra effort.

before the last frost date in your area. Transplant after the danger of frost has passed, and bury the plants up to their top leaves.

Tomatillo plants will sprawl, and they need a wide breadth of growing space (at least 4 feet) or they will soon take over your paths. Try to trellis them upwards, and keep them in bounds with some netting. Don't try to stake every vine, you'll soon run out of stakes, and your energies are better spent elsewhere.

To Harvest:

The husk of the tomatillo will grow large before the tomatillo. About two months after transplant, the husks will begin to fill with tomatillos, and the fruits will outgrow the husks.

Foes:

Pests rarely attack tomatillos.

Unless you douse every meal with a healthy serving of tomatillo salsa, you will probably only need two or three in your kitchen garden. Plant at least two for pollination, and share with friends if necessary.

SEED POSSIBILITIES:

Purple (H)—deep purple tomatillo with a sweet fruity flavor, much sweeter than green tomatillos; fruits measure 2" in diameter—*70-80 days*

Toma Verde (OP)—tart flavored green fruits; prolific and easy to care for; planes reach 3-4' round—*70 days*

Turnips—*Brassica rapa*

Ideal P.H.—5.5-6.8
Feed—light
Light requirements—full sun
Family—brassica

Friends:

Vegetables: beets, beans, carrots, lettuce, kohlrabi, peas, radishes, Swiss chard, and onions
Herbs: chamomile, dill, and fennel

FOR COMPANION PLANTING
See page 188 for an example of turnips interplanted with salad greens, peas, radishes, and carrots.

To Grow:

Seed turnips when the temperatures are between 40 and 70 degrees. I typically plant a few in the spring and many more towards fall. Fall crops will often produce better because the turnips will not bolt. Try mulching your turnips in the spring to slow them from bolting. Seeds should be placed at least 2 inches apart, and 1/2 inch in the soil when initially seeded—ultimately, each turnip should have 6 inches of space.

Rutabagas are actually a cross between turnips and cabbage, and they were originally called "Swedish Turnips."

Turnips require loose soil—their growth will be stunted if the soil is too compacted. To grow large roots, make sure turnips receive regular watering.

To Harvest:

Turnip greens are edible and quite tasty in a stir-fry. Freely harvest a few leaves from each root, but spare at least 3 or 4 for each turnip in the garden.

The turnips themselves can be harvested when they're young and tender, or they can be left in the garden through the fall. Pull them before they grow beyond 3 inches in diameter. If they grow too large, they might split, and they will toughen in texture. Thick mulch will keep them satisfied through frost, and they might even taste sweeter after they've had a light bite from the frosty weather.

Foes:

As brassica family members, turnips are subjected to the typical foes. See page 140 and 142 for more details. Flea beetles also attack turnip greens; however, the beetles will be easily confused by companion planted herbs or flowers.

Turnips do not grow well with potatoes, and there is conflicting evidence regarding whether they should be paired with other members of the brassica family.

SEED POSSIBILITIES:
Golden Ball (OP)—light yellow turnips, noted for their sweet flavor; sweet flavor in the greens also—*45-55 days*
Purple Top White (H)—classically colored turnips with purple tops and white bottoms; pull them when they reach 3-4" in diameter; the roots have a sweet, mild flavor and the greens are also edible—*55 days*
White Egg (OP)—sweet and mild flavor; greens will grow up to a foot and a half in height; a favorite of southern gardeners—*45-55 days*

Carrots make a good companion for turnip plants.

Jerusalem artichokes at midseason

Artichoke flowers

Chapter 11

COMPANION PLANTING WITH PERENNIAL EDIBLES

Artichokes—*Cynara cardunculus var. scolymus*

Perennial—zones 7-10
Ideal P.H.—6.5-8.0
Feed—heavy
Light requirements—full sun
Family—asteraceae

Friends:

Vegetables and Fruits: lettuce, radishes, onions, and strawberries
Flowers and Herbs: chives and lavender

> **FOR COMPANION PLANTING**
> Plant artichokes with beneficial flowers and perennial odorous herbs that repel aphids. Artichokes are quite decorative, so they can also be planted in the front flower gardens.

To Grow:

Artichokes grow best in areas of the country with temperate climates and favor temperatures between 50 and 70 degrees. Fortunately, with the right attention, artichokes can also be tricked into sending up sweet artichoke buds in many climate zones.

To acquire your own artichokes, try to find a friend who has an artichoke plant that needs dividing. If the plants are divided every three years, they can last up to 15 years in total. In early spring, gently dig up the plant by the roots. Divide by following the separate shoots of green.

Artichokes can also be started with seeds. Seeds should be planted at least 6 to 8 weeks before the last frost date and 10 to 12 weeks in more northern climates.

In their first year, artichokes produce buds inconsistently, and they appear later in the growing season—most often in early fall.

Artichoke seeds are often noted for their genetic variability and aren't always considered reliable. About 20 percent of artichoke seeds will not prove true.

Like flowering brassicas, the first flower on the artichoke is the largest.

To Harvest:

Artichokes will survive freezing temperatures, but the plants can die if it drops below 20 degrees. To keep the plants alive through the winter in cooler climates, cut the leaves until the plant measures one foot in height. Mulch the plant with a thick layer of chopped leaves or straw, and make sure to cover it completely. Drape the plants with burlap or a tarp and tuck them in for the winter. In zones 8 or warmer, just cut the plant down to ground level.

Foes:

As noted, artichokes are one of the favorite snacks of aphids. If you happen to spot ants climbing your artichokes, it's an indication that aphids are also feasting on your plants. To attract insects that will eat the aphids, tuck some flowers in the spaces between your artichoke plants.

SEED POSSIBILITIES:

Green Globe (OP)—a classic variety, these plants reach 4' in diameter and produce 3-4 heads; this hardy variety often remains productive for 5 years—*85 days*

Imperial Star (OP)—this variety grows up to 3' tall and will produce 1 or 2 primary bulbs, and then up to 7 extra along the sides; the buds are more common on this plant within the first year, so it's better for those in colder climates—*85 days*

Violetta di Chioggia (H)—an Italian heirloom, this plant produces beautiful purple artichokes that show more tolerance to climate variation; a perennial in zones 6 and above—*85 days*

Asparagus—*Asparagus officinalis*

Perennial—zones 3-8
Ideal P.H.—6.5-7.0
Feed—heavy
Light requirements—full sun
Family—asparagaceae

Friends:

Vegetables and Fruits: beets, carrots, lettuce, tomatoes, rhubarb, spinach, and strawberries
Flowers and Herbs: basil, cosmos, coriander, dill, and parsley

To Grow:

Asparagus is an obvious choice for anyone who knows they will be on the same plot of land for a number of years. Once established, asparagus can grow in the same bed for at least 20 years. It's an obvious choice for any gardener, as long as they have the room available. To plant the crowns, dig a trench that measures at least 6 inches deep. Leave room in the trench to shape a small mound of soil. If you've planted the asparagus in a row, just shape one long mound following the length of the trench. Place each crown sideways on the top of the mound with a distance of 15 inches between

---

FOR COMPANION PLANTING

Some companion planters establish perennial vegetable gardens, and they will interplant their rhubarb with asparagus and strawberries. Asparagus is also known to be a friend to the tomato plant. Its roots will emit a chemical (trichodorus) that will defend the tomatoes from attack by harmful nematodes. In turn, tomatoes contain a chemical called solanine, and it will drive away asparagus beetles. Asparagus also grows happily with spinach, carrots, lettuce, or beets.

In the first two months of the growing season, lettuce or spinach can be interplanted between the asparagus rows. Once the early spring greens bolt, beets or carrots can be companion planted for a fall crop.

Asparagus fronds that are not picked in early spring grow into tall fernlike foliage. Cosmos and dill have a similar appearance and will blend well with the asparagus plant. Basil and parsley also work well with asparagus.

Cosmos and asparagus ferns

each crown. Cover the crowns with two inches of soil, and gradually add more soil once you spot the tiny fronds.

The first year asparagus is planted, the fronds will only grow to a few feet in height. To prevent weeds from overtaking the fronds, surround them with a delicate layer of mulch as they appear. Pine needles intermixed with grass clippings or chopped leaves works well.

To Harvest:

The first year don't pick any of the fronds—allow them to grow into ferns. The asparagus fronds will be small and skinny, like miniature versions of mature asparagus. Although it might be an odd word to describe a vegetable, they're really cute.

The second year one can pick a few fronds, but most gardeners wait until the third year before picking. I've developed a little rule regarding picking that seems to work really well. I only harvest the thicker spears the first few years. Any little skinny spears that grow are left to fern. When picking your first fresh spears, cut them just below the surface of the soil.

Eventually, after a few years of growth, an asparagus bed will provide fresh asparagus from 6 to 8 weeks.

Foes:

The Asparagus Beetle—The asparagus beetle is the pest responsible for most asparagus damage. It measures a mere 1/4 of an inch and is marked by a black body with clear white spots and a bright red head with short antenna. The beetles will overwinter in the hollow stems of picked asparagus fronds, and then produce new generations that feed on the asparagus throughout the season. Their damage will become apparent when new asparagus start to bend over while still growing. Parasitic wasps attack asparagus beetles, so plant dill and parsley to entice the wasps.

Asparagus tends not to grow well with alliums.

SEED POSSIBILITIES:

Asparagus is generally purchased through a mail order, and it comes in the form of crowns. Look for hybrid varieties that include only male crowns. Those with female crowns will spend some of their energy producing little red berries and less energy producing crowns.

Jersey Knight (F1)—an all male variety of asparagus that has shown hardiness in cold climates; produces well in clay soil

Mary Washington (H)—a classic variety; reliably produces uniform green spears; a distinct asparagus taste; has demonstrated resistance to asparagus rust

Purple Passion (F1)—a purple variety of asparagus, noted for its sweet taste

Perennial Onions

Ideal P.H.—6.0-7.5
Feed—light
Light requirements—full sun
Family—allium

Perennial onions include Egyptian onions (or walking onions), potato onions, shallots, and bulbing leeks. With each variation, the onions will multiply to produce new bulbs.

FOR COMPANION PLANTING

Use perennial bulbs as protectors to ward off pests from more susceptible edibles. I have a few bulbs scattered all around my yard, near any plants that might need a bit of armor. Some are planted near my fruit trees, others protect my rose bushes, a few congregate near the perennial bed, and I've even snuck a few within the front flowerbeds.

To Grow:

Although perennial onions do not grow as large as annuals, they are largely unsusceptible to disease, and their reliability each season is appreciated. Perennial onions need to be planted in the fall, but they will grow most anywhere, and are not divided into "long-day" and "short-day" categories. If you wish to add some to your garden (and you should), buy them as cured bulbs, and plant them in a spot where they can multiply in the spring season.

Egyptian "walking" onions will naturally fall to the ground once the bulblets form on the top. I prefer to remove the bulblets, and place them in a purposeful location for the next season.

Potato onions will multiply into new bulbs by summer. Some varieties will produce one new large bulb, while others can produce up to a dozen smaller bulbs.

Shallots are actually a variation of a bulbing onion; they usually have reddish skin and a bit of a garlicky kick in their taste that differentiates them from a multiplier onion. Shallots will not fare well if conditions are too wet, or too dry.

To Harvest:

Harvest some of the bulbs for use in your kitchen, but be sure to replant some around the garden to continue the harvest. Egyptian onions and potato onions both store well.

Horseradish—*Armoracia rusticana*

Perennial—zones 2-9
Ideal P.H.—5.5-7.5
Feed—light
Light requirements—full sun
Family—brassica

FOR COMPANION PLANTING

If you have the space, plant the horseradish in a little patch in your yard. Horseradish is not prone to attack by insect or animal, so the plant needs little protection. Horseradish does grow quickly, and it's a challenge to eradicate it from a location once it's planted. Although some companion planters have suggested planting it near potatoes, it grows too quickly to make an effective companion in the ground. Instead, try planting the roots in a large pot. The pot can be located near the potatoes and relocated each year as the potatoes are rotated around the garden.

To Grow:

Horseradish is usually grown from actual horseradish root. Pick up some roots from the local farmer's market, or order a few through the mail. The roots can be planted as soon as the soil thaws in early spring. Place the roots in the ground at a 45-degree angle. The cutting edge of the root should measure approximately 2 inches below the soil's surface. To stimulate root production, once a generous amount of leaves appear above the soil, trim them back so that only a few are left for each crown.

Horseradish leaves will grow three to four feet tall, and the roots will spread.

To Harvest:

Younger roots can be harvested on an as-needed basis throughout the summer. The rest can be harvested once a frost kills the leaves. The horseradish flavor is much more pungent after frost, so consider harvesting earlier if you prefer a milder flavor.

Rhubarb—*Rheum rhabarbarum*

Perennial—zones 2-8
Ideal P.H.—6.0-6.8
Feed—light
Light requirements—full sun
Family—buckwheat

FOR COMPANION PLANTING

Rhubarb is virtually pest and disease free, so it can be planted on the outskirts of the garden. I have mine planted outside the garden fence as a border on the east side. Although the red stalks can make attractive foliage in the spring, the leaves will become ragged over summer, so it's best to keep rhubarb away from decorative flower beds.

There has been no research regarding rhubarb's companion planting capabilities, but I've planted some perennial herbs and flowers around the base.

To Grow:

Plant rhubarb crowns 2 to 3 inches below the soil line. Add some aged manure or compost with the new roots. Each crown should be planted at least 3 feet away from any other plants. A newly transplanted rhubarb plant will collapse within a day if it's not kept well watered. Be sure to water new transplants often.

Rhubarb favors loose, well-drained soil. Mulch the plants with grass clippings or chopped leaves, and add a layer of compost once a year.

Rhubarb is one of the first plants to sprout from the soil in spring.

Rhubarb plants

To Harvest:

Give your rhubarb plant a full year before harvesting any stalks. Harvest only a few the second year. The rhubarb stalks will gradually increase in width. In the third year, half the plant can be harvested a few times each season. To harvest, swiftly pull the chosen stalk from the ground. Always remove any flowering stalks at first sight. When harvesting, break the leaves from the stalks, and layer them around any nearby plants as mulch. The leaves are poisonous and should not be ingested.

Every four to five years the plants will need to be divided or trimmed.

Foes:

Rhubarb isn't attacked by anything of significance.

SEED POSSIBILITIES:
The *MacDonald* variety is probably the variety most often available commercially. It has bright red stalks that hold their color when cooked. The classic *Victoria* heirloom variety of rhubarb has thick green stalks that grow with vigor. *German Wine* is known for its sweet flavor.

Rhubarb and chives

Strawberries—*Fragaria x ananassa*

Perennial zones—(depends on the variety, most fall within zones 4-8)
Ideal P.H.—6.0-6.5
Feed—heavy
Light requirements—full sun
Family—rosaceae

Friends:

Vegetables: lettuce, beans, onions, radishes, and spinach
Flowers and Herbs: coriander, borage, and dill

FOR COMPANION PLANTING

Alpine strawberries can be planted in a perennial bed with other perennial vegetables like asparagus and rhubarb.

Strawberry plants that grow runners work better when planted in a single row down the center of a bed. I prefer to interplant June-bearing strawberries with low growing crops like lettuce and spinach. A scientific study indicated that interplanting strawberries with lettuce, onions, or radishes actually seemed to increase the productivity of the bed in total. Strawberries also produce well when they have borage as a companion, and borage is also reputed to repel pests.

Harvested strawberries

A strawberry patch

To Grow:

Plant strawberries in a raised bed to ensure that they are in well-drained soil. Strawberry plants have extremely shallow roots and those in newly established beds require regular watering to prevent wilt. New additions can be planted in early spring. The roots should be set slightly above the level of the ground. Space each plant approximately 18 inches apart.

Mulch around the plants to prevent root competition and to keep the plants moist. The plants will also need a protective blanket of mulch during the winter months to prevent any damage from the freezing temperatures.

Foes:

Sometimes, birds peck at ripe strawberries, nipping a small hole in each fruit just to leave their mark. I've found that I can prevent most damage by picking twice a day. You can also try row covers or hanging reflective CDs nearby. Most birds peck at fruit because they're thirsty, so a birdbath can also prevent damage.

Brassica plants, particularly cabbage, are said not to companion well with strawberries.

Even though the plants may start in rows, the runners will rapidly change the layout of the bed. Try to create some structure by guiding the runners in a zig-zag pattern. Remove at least half of the runners each year to focus the energy of the plants on fruit production. Every three years, transfer some of the runners to a new bed to start again. To keep a continuous supply of strawberries in my kitchen, I build a new bed every two years from existing runners.

To Harvest:

You won't have any strawberries the first season. Pinch the blossoms as they appear, and cut back half of the runners to promote an ample strawberry harvest in the second year. It's easy to spot a ripe strawberry—the bright red flesh stands out against the green foliage.

SEED POSSIBILITIES:

June-bearing strawberries grow the largest fruit, but the season lasts for only three weeks. *Everbearing* strawberries set fruit once in the spring, and they will set fruit again at least two more times during the growing season, though the fruit are much smaller in quantity. *Alpine* strawberries are the tiniest, but they will grow from spring until fall

Jerusalem Artichokes/Sunchokes— *Helianthus tuberosus*

Perennial—zones 3-10
Ideal P.H.—6.0-6.7
Feed—light
Light requirements—full sun to partial shade
Family—sunflower

FOR COMPANION PLANTING

Jerusalem artichokes will grow into a wall of greenery 10 feet tall, so they belong on the north side of the garden. Pole beans can be interplanted in front of them, and the Jerusalem artichokes will act as a natural trellis. They can also be planted as a windbreak, just avoid blocking the sun.

I've planted them as a patch in the yard. I then mow the plot on the outside edge to stop the artichokes from traveling beyond the intended space.

Above the ground, the tubers will sprout extremely tall sunflower-like foliage.

To Grow:

Jerusalem artichokes grow easily, but they prefer loose soil. They should be planted in early spring, once the soil can be worked. They really don't need extra care or fertilizer; it will only cause them to spread faster and more furiously. Plant each tuber 4 inches below the surface of the soil, and separate each by at least 16 inches.

Once the plants bloom, the flowers should be removed from the plants to propel the energy of the plants towards tuber production.

> Jerusalem artichokes are crisp, nutty tasting tubers that are native to Central and North America. Some people find that they have trouble digesting artichoke tubers, so roast a panful before making them a permanent fixture in your garden landscape.

To Harvest:

Wait until after the first hard frost before harvesting your Jerusalem artichokes from the soil. In warmer climates, the artichokes can be dug in the middle of the winter months. Like sweet potatoes, the tubers should be dug slowly and patiently. Use a digging fork to loosen the soil and your hands to dig the tubers out one by one. The tubers can be buried up to a foot deep, so take your time.

Like horseradish, some of the tubers won't make it out of the ground, and they'll turn into the new crop for the next year.

Foes:

Jerusalem artichokes don't really have any garden foes. They're largely disease and pest free. If a dog finds them, they will sometimes dig for a snack.

SEED POSSIBILITIES:

The simplest way to find seed tubers suitable for your climate is to pick up a few at the local farmer's market.

To Conclude:

Some gardeners have cast aside the term "companion planting" in favor of more modern names like "polyculture" or "inter-planting" or "edible landscaping." Companion planting has been derided as too folksy or unscientific. Gardeners may be perplexed by a companion gardener's jubilant anthropomor-phism of plants and flowers. Suggesting that one plant "likes" the companion of another can come across as antiquated.

Maybe I'm just less sensitive to specificity, but I feel that the name change is unnecessary and serves to confuse those who have tried to understand the gardening world, only to be put off by the semantic arguments of gardeners who dug too deeply into a cavern of word choice.

You can call this style of gardening whatever you wish. I wrote this book because I wanted to bring kitchen gardens back into our yards. I want to demonstrate the accessibility of "growing magic." Practically speaking, companion planting your kitchen garden makes your growing space more economi-cal and efficient. It ties you and your diet to nature in a way that can't be manufactured.

I hope I've convinced you to try companion planting, and if you've implemented the techniques described in this book, you should be well on your way.

SUGGESTED SEED COMPANIES

Specialty

East Branch Ginger
P.O. Box 321
Pittsboro, NC 27312
207-313-4358
http://www.eastbranchginger.com/

Filaree Garlic Farm
182 Conconully Highway
Okanogan, WA 98840
509-422-6940
http://www.filareefarm.com/

Garden Medicinals and Culinaries
P.O. Box 460
Mineral, VA 23117
540-872-8351
http://www.gardenmedicinals.com/

Gourmet Garlic Gardens
12300 FM 1176
Bangs, TX 76823
325-348-3049
http://www.gourmetgarlicgardens.com/

The Maine Potato Lady
P.O. Box 65
Guilford, ME 04443
207-717-5451
https://www.mainepotatolady.com/

Thomas Jefferson's Monticello
P.O. Box 318
Charlottesville, VA 22902
800-243-0743
http://www.monticelloshop.org/

The Thyme Garden Herb Company
20546 Alsea Highway
Alsea, OR 97324
541-487-8671
http://www.thymegarden.com/

The Vermont Wildflower Farm
P.O. Box 96
Charlotte, VT 05445
802-425-3641
http://www.vermontwildflowerfarm.com/

General

Adaptive Seeds
25079 Brush Creek Road
Sweet Home, OR 97386
541-367-1105
http://www.adaptiveseeds.com/

Annie's Heirloom Seeds
P.O. Box 467
Beaver Island, MI 49782
800-313-9140
http://www.anniesheirloomseeds.com/

Baker Creek Heirloom Seeds
2278 Baker Creek Road
Mansfield, MO 65704
417-924-8917
http://www.rareseeds.com/

BBB Seeds
6595 Odell Place, Unit G
Boulder, CO 80301
303-530-1222
http://www.bbbseed.com/

Botanical Interests, Inc.
660 Compton Street
Broomfield, CO 80020
877-821-4340
https://www.botanicalinterests.com/

Bountiful Gardens
1712-D South Main Street
Willits, CA 95490-4400
707-459-6410
http://www.bountifulgardens.org/

Circa Plants
66 South Orchard Street
Logan, OH 43138
740-603-6139
http://www.circaplants.com/

Clear Creek Seeds
P.O. Box 703
Hulbert, OK 74441
918-386-0546
http://www.clearcreekseeds.com/

D. Landreth Seed Company
60 East High Street, Building #4
New Freedom, PA 17349
800-654-2407
http://www.landrethseeds.com/

Fedco Seeds
P.O. Box 520
Waterville, ME 04903
207-426-9900
http://www.fedcoseeds.com/

Fruition Seeds
5920 County Road 33,
Naples, NY 14424
585-300-0699
http://www.fruitionseeds.com/

Foundroot Seeds
P.O. Box 289
Palmer, AK 99645
907-414-3077
http://www.foundroot.com/

High Mowing Organic Seeds
76 Quarry Road
Wolcott, VT 05680
802-472-6174
http://www.highmowingseeds.com/

Hudson Valley Seed Library
484 Mettacahonts Road
Accord, NY 12404
845-204-8769
http://www.seedlibrary.org/

Humble Seed
P.O. Box 8017
Ann Arbor, MI 48107
877-956-7333
http://www.humbleseed.com/

Johnny's Selected Seeds
P.O. Box 299
Waterville, ME 04903
877-564-6697
http://www.johnnyseeds.com/

John Scheepers Kitchen Garden Seeds
23 Tulip Drive
Bantam, CT 06750
860-567-6086
http://www.kitchengardenseeds.com/

Livingston Seed
830 Kinnear Road
Columbus, OH 43212
800-848-2970
http://www.livingstonseed.com/

Marianna's Heirlooms
7485 North 1 Road
Copemish, MI 49625
https://www.mariannasheirloomseeds.com/

Mountain Valley Seed Co.
455 West 1700 South
Salt Lake City, UT 84115
801-486-0480
http://www.mvseeds.com/

Native Seeds
3584 East River Road
Tucson, AZ 85718
520-622-0830
http://www.nativeseeds.org/

Nichols Garden Nursery
1190 Old Salem Road NE
Albany, OR 97321
800-422-3985
https://www.nicholsgardennursery.com/

Organic Sanctuary

1319 Cochran Road
Geneva, FL 32732
321-591-4794
http://www.organicsanctuary.com/

Osborne Seed Company, LLC

2428 Old Highway 99 South Road
Mount Vernon, WA 98273
360-424-7333
http://www.osborneseed.com/

Peaceful Valley Farm & Garden Supply

P.O. Box 2209
Grass Valley, CA 95945
888-784-1722
http://www.groworganic.com/

Pinetree Garden Seeds

P.O. Box 300
New Gloucester, ME 04260
207-926-3400
https://www.superseeds.com/

Renee's Garden

6060 Graham Hill Road
Felton, CA 95018
888-880-7228
http://www.reneesgarden.com/

Restoration Seeds

1133 Old Highway 99 S.
Ashland, OR 97520
541-201-2688
http://www.restorationseeds.com/

Salt Spring Seeds

Box 444, Ganges P.O.
Salt Spring Island
BC, V8K 2W1 Canada
250-537-5269
http://www.saltspringseeds.com/

Sand Hill Preservation Center

1878 230th Street
Calamus, IA 52729
563-246-2299
http://www.sandhillpreservation.com/

Seeds of Change

P.O. Box 4908
Rancho Dominguez, CA 90220
888-762-7333
http://www.seedsofchange.com/

Seed Savers Exchange

3094 North Winn Road
Decorah, IA 52101
563-382-5990
http://www.seedsavers.org/

Southern Exposure Seed Exchange

P.O. Box 460
Mineral, VA 23117
540-894-9480
http://www.southernexposure.com/

Sow True Seed

146 Church Street
Asheville, NC 28801
828-254-0708
http://www.sowtrueseed.com/

Sustainable Seed Company

P.O. Box 38
Covelo CA, 95428
877-620-SEED
http://www.sustainableseedco.com/

Terroir Seeds

P.O. Box 4995
Chino Valley AZ 86323
888-878-5247
http://www.underwoodgardens.com/

Territorial Seed Company

P.O. Box 158
Cottage Grove, OR 97424
800-626-0866
http://www.territorialseed.com/

Uprising Seeds

2208 Iron Street
Bellingham, WA 98225
360-778-3749
http://www.uprisingorganics.com/

Vesey's Seeds
P.O. Box 9000
Calais, ME 04619-6102
800-363-7333
http://www.veseys.com/

Victory Seed Company
P.O. Box 192
Molalla, OR 97038
503-829-3126
http://www.victoryseeds.com/

Wild Garden Seed
P.O. Box 1509
Philomath, OR 97370
541-929-4068
http://www.wildgardenseed.com/

Wood Prairie Farm
49 Kinney Road
Bridgewater, ME 04735
800-829-9765
http://www.woodprairie.com/

SCIENTIFIC STUDIES UTILIZED

Amarawardana, Lakmali, Premaratne Bandara, Vijaya Kumar, Jan Pettersson, Velemir Ninkovic, Robert Glinwood. "Olfactory Response of Myzus persicae (Homoptera: Aphididae) to Volatiles from Leek and Chive: Potential for Intercropping with Sweet Pepper, Section." *Soil & Plant Science* 57 (2007): 87-91.

Asare-Bediako, E., A.A. Addo-Quaye and A. Mohammed. "Control of Diamondback Moth *Plutella xylostella* on Cabbage *Brassica oleracea var capitata* using Intercropping with Non-Host Crops." *American Journal of Food Technology* 5 (2010): 269-274.

Booij, C. J. H., J. Noorlander, J. Theunissen. "Intercropping Cabbage with Clover: Effects on Ground Beetles." *Biological Agriculture & Horticulture* 15 (1997): 261-268.

Fininsa, Chemeda. "Effect of Intercropping Bean with Maize on Bean Common Bacterial Blight and Rust Diseases," *International Journal of Pest Management* 42 (1996): 51-54.

"Geraniums and Begonias: New Research on Old Garden Favorites." *Agricultural Research* (2010): 18-19.

Hooks, C. R. R., Hinds, J., Zobel, E. and Patton, T., "Impact of Crimson Clover Dying Mulch on Two Eggplant Insect Herbivores." *Journal of Applied Entomology* 137 (2013): 170-180.

Jankowska, Beata. "Effect of Intercropping White Cabbage with French Marigold and Pot Marigold on Diamondback Moth." 73 (2010): 107-117.

Jankowska, Beata, Elżbieta Jędrszczyk, Małgorzata Poniedziałek. "Effect of Intercropping Carrot *Daucus carota L.* with French Marigold *Tagetes patula nana L.* and Pot Marigold *Calendula officinalis L.* on the Occurrence of Some Pests and Quality of Carrot Yield." *Acta Agrobotanica* 65 (2012): 133-138.

Karlidag, Huseyin and Ertan Yildirim. "Strawberry Intercropping with Vegetables for Proper Utilization of Space and Resources." *Journal of Sustainable Agriculture* 33 (2009): 107-116.

Moreau, Tara L., P. R. Warman, J. Hoyle. "An Evaluation of Companion Planting and Botanical Extracts as Alternative Pest Controls for the Colorado Potato Beetle." *Biological Agriculture & Horticulture* 23 (2006): 351-370.

Schultz, Brian, Cruz Phillips, Peter Rosset and John Vandemeer. "An Experiment in Intercropping Cucumbers and Tomatoes in Southern Michigan." *Scientia Horticulturae*, 18 (1982): 1-8.

Uvah, I. I. I. and Coaker, T. H., "Effect of Mixed Cropping on some Insect Pests of Carrots and Onions." *Entomologia Experimentalis et Applicata* 36 (1984): 159-167.

Yildirm, Ertan and Ismail Guvenc. "Intercropping Based on Cauliflower: More Productive, Profitable and Highly Sustainable." *Journal of Sustainable Agriculture* 23 (2006): 29-44.

Yu, Jing Quan. "Allelopathic Suppression of *Pseudomonas solanacearum* Infection of Tomato (*Lycopersicon esculentum*) in a Tomato-Chinese Chive (*Allium tuberosum*) Intercropping System." *Journal of Chemical Ecology* 25 (1999): 2409-2417.

Wanga, Koon-Hui, Cerruti R Hooksa, and Antoon Ploegb. "Protecting Crops from Nematode Pests: Using Marigold as an Alternative to Chemical Nematicides" Department of Plant and Environmental Protection Sciences, University of Hawaii at Mänoa Department of Nematology, University of California, Riverside Plant Disease, (2007): 1-6.

Flores-Sanchez, D., A. Pastor, E. A. Lantinga, W. A. H. Rossing, M. J. Kropff. "Exploring Maize-Legume Intercropping Systems in Southwest Mexico." *Agroecology and Sustainable Food Systems* 37 (2013): 739-761.

Makinde, Eyitayo A., Olukemi T. Ayoola, Esther A. Makinde. "Intercropping Leafy Greens and Maize on Weed Infestation, Crop Development, and Yield." *International Journal of Vegetable Science* 15 (2009): 402-411.

INDEX